VICTORY OR DEATH

A Wargamer's Guide to the American Revolution, 1775–1782

David C. Bonk

HELION &
COMPANY

Helion & Company Limited
Unit 8 Amherst Business Centre
Budbrooke Road
Warwick
CV34 5WE
England
Tel. 01926 499 619
Email: info@helion.co.uk
Website: www.helion.co.uk
Twitter: @helionbooks
Visit our blog http://blog.helion.co.uk/

Published by Helion & Company 2024
Designed and typeset by Mary Woolley, Battlefield Design (www.battlefield-design.co.uk)
Cover designed by Paul Hewitt, Battlefield Design (www.battlefield-design.co.uk)

Text © David C. Bonk 2024
Photographs © David C. Bonk 2024
Colour artwork by Patrice Courcelle © Helion & Company 2024
Maps by George Anderson © Helion & Company 2024

ISBN 978-1-804513-57-6

British Library Cataloguing-in-Publication Data.
A catalogue record for this book is available from the British Library.

For details of other military history titles published by Helion & Company Limited contact the above address or visit our website: http://www.helion.co.uk.

We always welcome receiving book proposals from prospective authors.

Contents

British battle line advancing. 28mm Old Glory figures.

1

Why the American Revolution?

My interest in historical miniatures wargaming extends back to the late 1960s when I was introduced to board wargames. My attention turned to miniatures in the early 1970s and while I still own and play boardgames, for the last 50 years I have collected and played historical miniatures wargames in a range of periods, using a wide variety of rules.

Although my initial period of interest was in Napoleonic wargaming, beginning in the mid-1970s, and in conjunction with the start of the celebration of the bicentennial of the American Revolution I began wargaming this period.

What I found then, which continues to be the case today, is a wide interest in the American Revolution among wargamers. Since I began miniatures wargaming the overall hobby has grown as reflected in the variety of range of miniatures and scales, covering almost every period of military history. Despite this expansion into other periods, the American Revolution continues to hold a solid interest among wargamers.

The American Revolutionary period has attracted the interest of a wide range of wargamers for a variety of reasons. The period features battles ranging from minor skirmishes to large set piece battles. The battles were fought over a wide variety of different terrain ranging from primitive frontier to cultivated farmland to dense primeval forests. The battles were fought in weather ranging from the bitter cold of Canada in winter to the intense heat and humidity of South Carolina during the summer. In addition to the historical engagements the period offers the opportunity to explore battles that might have taken place if different decisions had been made by the respective commanders.

For those wargamers interested in conducting broader campaigns to generate challenging tabletop battles, the American Revolution also offers several different options. These campaigns can differ in the size and composition of the opposing armies and the characteristics of the theatre of operations, ranging from more developed farming areas near large cities to sparely populated wilderness. The campaigns can be conducted in any season and will be impacted by the cold and snow of winter to sweltering heat and debilitating disease during the summer in southern colonies and tropical West Indies.

View from British lines of an American Revolution wargame using 40mm figures.

While most battles of the Revolution were fought by American Continental regiments pitted against British regulars, there were substantial differences in training and experience between units of the same army. Both armies were typically supplemented by militia and Loyalist units and the British actively recruited Provincial units which were better trained than most Loyalist units and performed at the same level as regular units. The American Revolution also involves large contingents of German units and French expeditionary armies, as well as Native American forces. The rich variety of unit types contributes to the interest in the period.

The focus of this guide will be on providing the historical background necessary to better understand the key elements of warfare during the American Revolution. The guide addresses topics relevant to miniatures wargaming. While it provides a broad overview of the military history of the war, the focus will be on the organisation, appearance and tactical doctrine of the opposing forces. In the case of the American Continental army there were several modifications to the organisation of infantry regiments over the course of the war. In addition, this book will provide information on the appearance of the armies, including uniform information. Just as the American regiments changed organisation there were also several changes to uniforms throughout the war.

British assault on American lines, using 40mm figures.

This guide will provide an overview of the American Revolution to establish a framework for the more detailed exploration of the armies that fought the war and the generals that led the armies into battle. The framework will also give wargamers a foundation to use in order to build their armies and decide whether to refight historical battles or simulate campaigns to generate new engagements. The guide will include examples of several historic engagements, provide information on possible 'what if' battles and offer examples of how campaigns can be used to generate interesting tabletop battles.

Unless otherwise noted, the photographs in the book are of 28mm and 40mm miniatures, buildings and terrain from the collections of the author and of Christopher Hughes of Sash and Sabre Miniatures. Thanks to Chris Hughes for the use of his extensive collection of both 28mm and 40mm figures. The majority of 28mm figures are Old Glory along with various other manufacturers as noted. The 40mm figures are a mix of Sash and Sabre, Triguard and Front Rank.

2

Strategic Overview

The British North American Colonies

In the aftermath of the French and Indian War the British in North America acquired vast new holdings, expanding westward to the Mississippi river and securing all of Canada. British North America was composed of the 13 colonies and the former French possessions to the north and northwest. These were divided into the provinces of Quebec and Nova Scotia, as well as the Island of Saint John, and the colony of Newfoundland and Prince Rupert's Land. To the west of the 13 colonies a large swath of land extending to the Mississippi River, was designated as the Indian Reserve. To the south the provinces of East and West Florida were also governed by Britain.

At the beginning of the American Revolution in 1775, the estimated population of the 13 colonies was approximately 2.33 million, which included slaves. The colonies themselves ranged in size from Virginia, the largest, with a population of 530,000, to Georgia, the smallest, with 27,000 residents. In addition, approximately 63,000 colonists lived in lands, mainly in the west and north, claimed by one of the original 13 colonies but that later were separated to create a new state. The city of Philadelphia boasted the largest municipal population with approximately 40,000 residents, followed by New York City (25,000), Boston (15,000), Charleston, South Carolina (12,000) and Newport, Rhode Island (11,000). By comparison, the population of Great Britain in 1776 was approximately eight million and London's population was 750,000.

With only about 10 percent of the population of the colonies residing in cities and towns, the bulk of colonists were concentrated in a swath from Maryland, through Eastern Pennsylvania, into New Jersey and along the coastline from New York City to Boston. A smaller concentration of population lived between Savannah, Georgia and Charleston, South Carolina.

In addition to the American colonies, Britain also had extensive holdings in the Caribbean and West Indies. Britain controlled Jamaica, Barbados, the Leeward Islands, Grenada, which included Tobago, Saint Vincent and Dominica. The last three were acquired from France as part of the Treaty of Paris of 1763, which ended the Seven Years' War. These islands represented a major economic resource, providing sugar and rum for export and maintained trade with the mainland colonies, particularly South Carolina.

Close by the British possessions were the islands controlled by France, Guadeloupe, Martinique and Saint Lucia in the Lesser Antilles. Denmark owned the islands of Saint John, Saint Croix and Saint Thomas while the Spanish occupied several islands including Cuba, Hispaniola and Trinidad.

While the lands acquired by the 1763 Treaty of Paris opened up vast new territories to be explored and resources to be exploited, they also added new demands on the British political and military establishments. The cost of the Seven Years' War to the British treasury was significant and had to be repaid. Added to that was the cost of administering their new North American domains. Whatever else the British government understood they were committed to the supposition that in order to regain financial stability, their American colonists would be required to bear a large share of the cost.

Beginning in 1764 with the Sugar Act, a series of unpopular taxes levied upon the American colonies led to widespread discontent and laid the foundation of grievances that would assert themselves in the coming revolution. The tax rebellions came to a head in December 1773 with the 'Boston Tea Party' where protesters destroyed tea valued at over 15,000 pounds sterling. In response the British Parliament passed a series of punitive measures, closing the port of Boston, annulling portions of the province's charter, restricting the assembly of residents at town meetings without approval by the Royal executive, and requiring the housing of British troops within Boston. In May 1774, Lieutenant General George Gage arrived in Boston to enforce the laws and on 1 June 1774 the Port Act went into effect. Gage, who had travelled to America in 1755, had fought in the French and Indian War and been appointed commander-in-chief of British armed forces in America in 1763.

The Port Act required that Boston be closed to any outside trade, and for a year the city had to be supported with supplies and food from sympathetic neighbouring colonies. Steadfast in their refusal to reimburse the British government for the cost of the tea destroyed, in 1773 the residents of Boston also saw Gage remove the seat of government to nearby Salem. After an unsuccessful attempt to constitute a General Assembly and Supreme Court in Salem, Gage returned to Boston while a Provincial Congress, composed of disaffected citizens, met in Concord. The groundwork for revolution had been laid.

Among the actions taken by the Provincial Congress was to reorganise the structure of the militia organisations. The Congress stipulated three types of militias. The minutemen would represent up to one-third of the overall militia forces and be organised around companies of 50 men, ready to respond on short notice. The minutemen were given priority with regard to equipment and received extra training. These companies were intended to be grouped together to compose regiments of 10 companies. Although the Provincial Congress formalised the militia organisation, individual colonies had already taken actions to strengthen their militia. Virginia, Maryland, Rhode Island and Massachusetts trained vigorously at formation drill and musketry. New Hampshire organised local militia in 1771, followed in 1772 by New York, while by 1774 Connecticut boasted a force of 20,000 organised into 18 regiments.

The regular militia companies were also organised along the lines of the minutemen, with regiments expected to be composed of between six and 15 companies. The 'alarm companies' were composed of older, younger or infirmed villagers. The size of the alarm

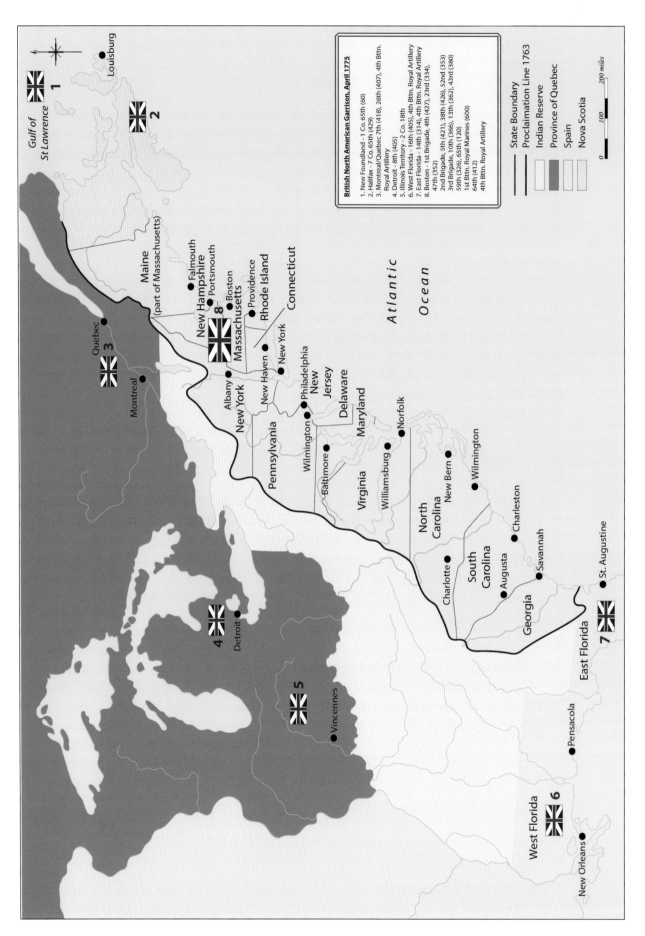

In 1775 North America was divided between British and Spanish holdings. Britain controlled the 13 colonies and Canada. The lands west of the colonial boundaries had been set aside for the Native American tribes, although colonial settlers continued to encroach into this area.

companies varied depending on the size of their home villages and were not considered part of the regular militia regiments.

At the beginning of 1774, 13 British regiments of foot and five companies of the 4th Battalion of the Royal Artillery were stationed in North America. These troops were deployed to provide security to the British possessions in Canada and Florida, as well as to protect the western frontier from Native American incursions. With the rise of tensions within the colonies and Gage's arrival in Boston, the balance of forces began to change. Gage requested and was granted four additional foot regiments along with a battalion of marines. By April 1775 Gage had collected 4,000 infantry, 600 marines and 300 Royal Artillery around Boston.

1775 Strategic Summary

In response to the unfolding crisis in Boston, the first Continental Congress met in Philadelphia on 5 September 1774. Representatives from 12 of the 13 states were in attendance. The Congress prepared and adopted a variety of petitions, including an address to the People of England and a Declaration of Rights, which outlined the Acts of Parliament the colonists found repugnant and refused to adhere to. To support the petitions, the Congress also proposed that a boycott of goods from Great Britain, Ireland and the West Indies be organised through the establishment of a Continental Association of colonial states. Although the petitions were ignored by both King George III and the British Parliament the rebellion continued to take shape.

In the face of increasing provocations, the British Parliament met in November 1774 and received an address from King George III, describing the actions in Massachusetts as 'a most daring spirit of resistance and disobedience'. Parliament responded by agreeing that a rebellion was brewing and that they would support whatever measures the king might take to re-establish his authority. The King then made a 'solemn assurance' to Parliament that 'the most speedy and effectual measures' would be taken. Towards that end an additional 6,000 troops were dispatched to Boston, raising the overall total to over 10,000.

Throughout the winter of 1774–1775 the Massachusetts militia organised in villages near Boston. In April, a British raid to destroy militia supplies at Lexington and Concord ended with the defeat of the British column. News of the British raid spread throughout the New England colonies and then through all the colonies. Within days several thousand militia gathered outside Boston and by early June approximately 15,000 men had assembled.

The American capture of British forts at Ticonderoga and Crown Point on 10 May resulted in the capture of almost 150 pieces of artillery and large quantities of ammunition. Much of this artillery was immediately sent to militia forces outside Boston.

On 17 June 1775, British forces in Boston attempted to drive Colonial forces from positions at Breeds Hill and Bunker Hill. The British finally captured Breeds Hill after three bloody assaults and forced the American evacuation of Bunker Hill.

In the aftermath of Bunker Hill, British General Gage, commander of British forces in the American colonies, cautioned that more resources were necessary including the

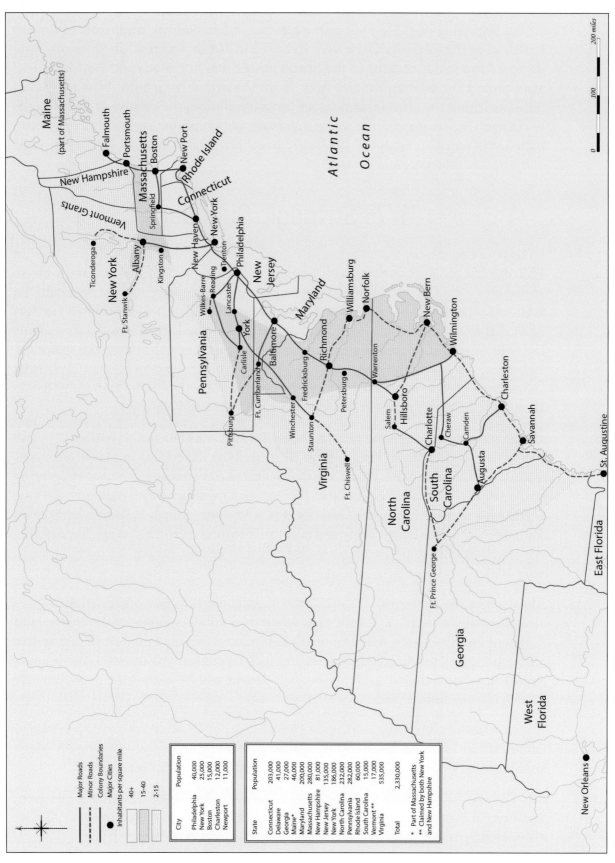

At the start of the American Revolution the islands of the West Indies were divided between Britain, France, Spain, the Netherlands and the Danes. With the entry of France into the war against Britain in 1778 the West Indies became an important theatre of war.

organisation of a large army. Parliament promised Gage 20,000 additional troops by the spring of 1776. In addition, the Governor of Canada, Major General Guy Carleton, was authorised to recruit Native American Indians and Canadians, while British officials in the colonies were directed to raise units of Loyalists. The British government approached Catherine the Great of Russia with a proposal to hire 20,000 Russian troops to serve in North America. Catherine rejected the offer. Negotiations were also initiated with several small German principalities to secure the services of their military units.

In July 1775, the American Congress agreed on two broad objectives; to drive the British out of Canada and contain Howe's army in Boston. General George Washington assumed overall command of the militia forces at Cambridge, Massachusetts on 2 July. In response to a report from Washington summarising the deficiencies of the American army, a Congressional committee recommended the organisation of a Continental Army, composed of 28 infantry regiments, supplemented by units of riflemen and artillery. Each regiment was to be composed of 728 men, uniformed in brown coats with distinctive facings for each colony.

On 27 July Congress appointed Major General Phillip Schuyler to command American forces in the Northern Department and directed him to evaluate the feasibility of an invasion of Canada. Schuyler and Brigadier General Montgomery advanced into Canada, besieging British forces at Saint John in early September. After a failed relief effort by British Major General Carleton, Saint John surrendered on 2 November and American forces captured Montreal on 13 November. As British forces retreated to Quebec, Colonel Benedict Arnold led a force through the Maine wilderness arriving at Quebec in early November. Joined by Montgomery's main force, the siege of Quebec lasted until late December. American forces assaulted the city on 31 December but were repulsed with Montgomery killed and Arnold wounded.

Throughout the summer and into the fall of 1775 both sides remained largely inactive. While Gage's men in Boston suffered from shortages of fresh provisions, Vice Admiral Samuel Graves came under severe criticism from Gage's senior commanders for his inability to protect supplies and safeguard British contact with England.

Gage was relieved of his command in October 1775 and after conferring with his successor, Lieutenant General William Howe, both concluded that the situation in Boston was untenable. They recommended the bulk of the army be withdrawn to New York and Long Island. Howe reported to the British Prime Minister, Lord North, and his cabinet that unless an army of 30,000 was organised the British might have to abandon the American colonies.

By November 1775, North expanded negotiations with various German princes for the purchase of their troops to serve in America. Near the end of 1775 approximately 10,000 troops embarked for North America.

American militia enlistments began expiring on 10 December and in response Washington initiated a programme of inducements, including cash payments, to encourage re-enlistments. Only 8,000 men remained in the army by the end of 1775 but recruitment campaigns in the New England states produced another 4,000 men during the early part of 1776. Despite this success, Congress refused to authorise enlistments longer than a year, although they did approve a six-month term.

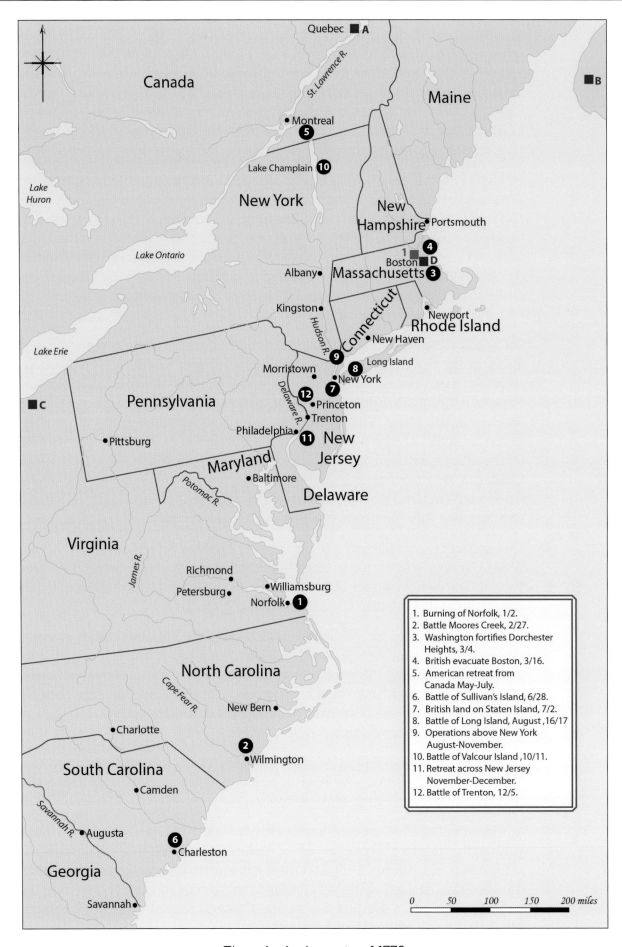

1. Burning of Norfolk, 1/2.
2. Battle Moores Creek, 2/27.
3. Washington fortifies Dorchester Heights, 3/4.
4. British evacuate Boston, 3/16.
5. American retreat from Canada May-July.
6. Battle of Sullivan's Island, 6/28.
7. British land on Staten Island, 7/2.
8. Battle of Long Island, August ,16/17
9. Operations above New York August-November.
10. Battle of Valcour Island ,10/11.
11. Retreat across New Jersey November-December.
12. Battle of Trenton, 12/5.

The principal events of 1776

1776 Strategic Events

1776 found the British firmly established in Boston while smaller detachments were posted in Newfoundland and on the western frontier and at Quebec. American forces were concentrated around Boston.

The new British commander, Lieutenant General William Howe, accepted that a lack of shipping would delay the evacuation of Boston until the spring.

British Members of Parliament also lamented the events at Boston, although Lord North's ruling party was unanimous in their commitment to carry out a military campaign to subdue the American rebels. During the summer of 1775, Lord North's government developed a strategy that included a blockade of the New England colonies in conjunction with the capture of New York and Rhode Island, followed by simultaneous advances along the Hudson River from Canada and New York. The plan also included an offensive in the southern colonies designed to encourage Loyalist sentiments.

Although sceptical of the southern operation, Howe assigned Major General Henry Clinton to capture Charleston in January 1776. North Carolina Loyalists were defeated at Moore's Creek in February while Clinton failed to capture Fort Sullivan in June and July.

Howe evacuated Boston in March, retiring to Halifax, Nova Scotia, where the British army reorganised and retrained. Howe sailed to New York in July, landing on Staten Island. Pausing briefly to wait for reinforcements, Howe crossed over to Long Island in late August and outmanoeuvred Washington off the Brooklyn Heights and drove the Americans back onto Manhattan Island.

In September Howe used the Royal Navy to land at Kips Bay and force the Americans to abandon New York City. After a series of small battles at Harlem Heights, Throngs Point and Pell's Point, Washington retreated to White Plains in late October. Howe confronted Washington at White Plains but after several days of manoeuvring, he retreated, allowing the Americans to retire over the Hudson River into New Jersey. The British captured Fort Washington on 16 November and pursued Washington's retreating army through New Jersey, forcing the Americans to cross the Delaware River into Pennsylvania.

After the British assumed winter quarters in late November, Washington struck at the German garrison at Trenton, New Jersey, on 26 December. Returning to New Jersey several days later, Washington was pursued by Lieutenant General Charles Cornwallis back to Trenton but successfully retired and defeated a British column at Princeton on 3 January before retreating to Morristown.

In Canada, the British pushed south from Quebec in May and American resistance slowly collapsed. General Carleton paused after capturing Saint John in June to construct ships to challenge the American fleet operating in Lake Champlain under the command of Colonel Benedict Arnold. In October, the British defeated Arnold's small fleet off Valcour Island but suspended offensive operations without capturing Fort Ticonderoga due the onset of winter.

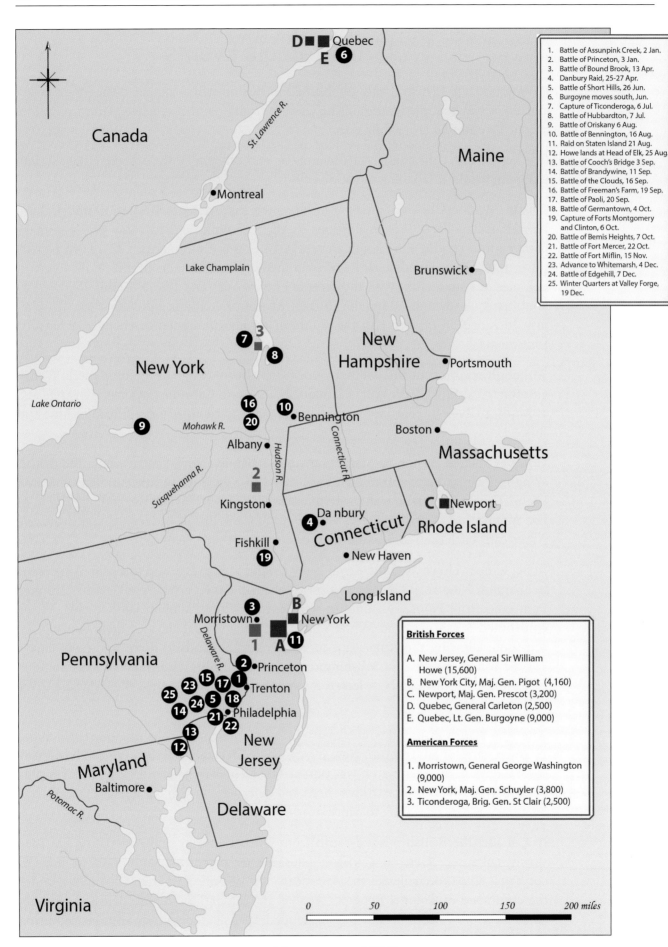

1. Battle of Assunpink Creek, 2 Jan.
2. Battle of Princeton, 3 Jan.
3. Battle of Bound Brook, 13 Apr.
4. Danbury Raid, 25-27 Apr.
5. Battle of Short Hills, 26 Jun.
6. Burgoyne moves south, Jun.
7. Capture of Ticonderoga, 6 Jul.
8. Battle of Hubbardton, 7 Jul.
9. Battle of Oriskany 6 Aug.
10. Battle of Bennington, 16 Aug.
11. Raid on Staten Island 21 Aug.
12. Howe lands at Head of Elk, 25 Aug.
13. Battle of Cooch's Bridge 3 Sep.
14. Battle of Brandywine, 11 Sep.
15. Battle of the Clouds, 16 Sep.
16. Battle of Freeman's Farm, 19 Sep.
17. Battle of Paoli, 20 Sep.
18. Battle of Germantown, 4 Oct.
19. Capture of Forts Montgomery and Clinton, 6 Oct.
20. Battle of Bemis Heights, 7 Oct.
21. Battle of Fort Mercer, 22 Oct.
22. Battle of Fort Miflin, 15 Nov.
23. Advance to Whitemarsh, 4 Dec.
24. Battle of Edgehill, 7 Dec.
25. Winter Quarters at Valley Forge, 19 Dec.

British Forces

A. New Jersey, General Sir William Howe (15,600)
B. New York City, Maj. Gen. Pigot (4,160)
C. Newport, Maj. Gen. Prescot (3,200)
D. Quebec, General Carleton (2,500)
E. Quebec, Lt. Gen. Burgoyne (9,000)

American Forces

1. Morristown, General George Washington (9,000)
2. New York, Maj. Gen. Schuyler (3,800)
3. Ticonderoga, Brig. Gen. St Clair (2,500)

The events of 1777

1777 Strategic Events

After the British failure to defeat Washington's army in late 1776, the British recognised the war would require additional resources and a more comprehensive strategy. Howe distributed his forces throughout New Jersey to monitor Washington at Morristown while maintaining sizeable detachments in New York City and Newport, Rhode Island. British forces in Canada were centred at Quebec while Fort Ticonderoga remained in American control. Washington's main army, which had shrunk to several thousand men, remained at Morristown with small detachments deployed to guard the Hudson Highlands in New York.

A revival of French interest in providing support to the Americans with news of British defeats at Trenton and Princeton, coupled with the arrival of Benjamin Franklin in Paris at the end of 1776, caught the attention of the British government. In response, six more warships and 6,000 additional troops were slated for dispatch to America.

In late 1776 Howe submitted a plan for the 1777 campaign. While maintaining a garrison at New York City, Howe's plan envisioned a sizeable demonstration towards Philadelphia and an attack on Newport and Providence, Rhode Island, while also threatening Boston. To support the anticipated offensive in Canada, Howe also proposed a thrust north from New York along the Hudson River.

After successfully lobbying for command of the British offensive from Canada, Lieutenant General John Burgoyne suggested once the forces had concentrated and Fort Ticonderoga was captured, he would advance east to either support the effort against Newport or embark his army to join the attack on Philadelphia.

Howe revised his plan in February proposing to now focus exclusively on the capture of Philadelphia, eliminating both the attack on Newport and the drive up the Hudson River to meet the Canadian army. The British government approved Howe's revised plan while at the same time assuming that Howe would capture Philadelphia quickly before moving north to support Burgoyne's advance from Canada. For his part Howe had abandoned any thought of direct support for Burgoyne but suggested a smaller force from the New York garrison might be dispatched to assist the invasion.

Before initiating his offensive against Philadelphia, Howe sought to defeat Washington's army, still deployed around Morristown. Morristown, protected by the Watchung Mountains, provided Washington with a secure base and supported the continuing harassment of British foraging parties by New Jersey militia. In April, Lieutenant General Cornwallis, with 4,000 troops, attempted to surprise Major General Benjamin Lincoln's division at Boundbrook. Lincoln's forces escaped and retired in disorder. Howe also ordered a raid on the American supply base at Danbury, Connecticut.

In June Howe sought again to bring Washington's army into battle by advancing from New Brunswick, New Jersey, towards Somerset Courthouse. Both Americans and British assumed this was the beginning of the British advance towards Philadelphia but after an initial skirmish at Short Hill, rather than continue to advance Howe settled down for two days, building fortifications. Disappointed that Washington was unwilling engage in battle Howe ordered a return to New York, to the surprise and consternation of many of his officers.

At the same time, Burgoyne advanced south from Canada, capturing Fort Ticonderoga after a short siege in early July. Continuing to march down the Saint Lawrence River, Burgoyne's forces raided Hubbardton, Vermont. In August, a force of Loyalists and Native Americans under Colonel St Leger ambushed a large American militia force at Oriskany, New York while a raid against Bennington, Vermont ended in a German defeat.

After receiving news of Burgoyne's successful capture of Fort Ticonderoga, Howe ordered his army aboard transports and sailed from New York on 23 July. Unsure of Howe's destination, Washington deployed his army to protect both Philadelphia and American positions along the Hudson River.

After a brief appearance at the mouth of the Delaware River on 30 July, Howe finally landed at Head of Elk on 24 August. After pausing to reorganise and establish a supply base, Howe moved north, pushing aside an American force at Cooch's Bridge on 3 September. Washington retired towards Philadelphia and deployed his army along the Brandywine River. On 11 September Howe outflanked the American positions and forced Washington to retreat.

Rather than strike directly at Philadelphia, the British marched through Pennsylvania for two weeks. Brigadier General Anthony Wayne's command was ambushed at Paoli Tavern and Washington retired across the Schuykill River. After feigning an attack on the Continental supply base at Reading on 21 September, Howe doubled back and entered Philadelphia on 26 September. The American Forts Mercer and Mifflin on the Delaware River prevented the Royal Navy from providing needed supplies.

AWI wargame in progress using 40mm figures and terrain.

In Canada, Burgoyne cut his supply lines and endeavoured to push south and capture Albany on 13 September. With only a month of supplies, Burgoyne sent a message to Lieutenant General Clinton in New York requesting he attack north. While Burgoyne paused, Major General Gates raised additional militia and fortified his position at Bemis Heights. Burgoyne bumped into Horatio Gates' position and fought the battle of Freeman's Farm on 17 September. Burgoyne failed to force Gates to retreat and after learning the British supply bases at Fort Ticonderoga were under threat and the supply fleet on Lake George had been destroyed, again requested Clinton's help to dislodge the Americans.

Washington struck back at Howe's forces outside Philadelphia at Germantown on 4 October, while Lieutenant General Clinton attempted to support Burgoyne's stalled offensive by advancing up the Hudson River on 3 October, capturing Fort Montgomery and Fort Clinton, but failed to reach Albany. Burgoyne was defeated on 7 October at Bemis Heights before surrendering at Saratoga on 17 October.

Howe captured the Delaware River forts in late October before making one final attempt to bring Washington's army into a decisive battle at Whitemarsh and Edgehill in early December. The year ended with news of Burgoyne's surrender reaching London in early December, while Howe settled into winter quarters at Philadelphia. Washington stayed near Philadelphia, establishing winter quarters at Valley Forge.

1778 Strategic Events

1778 found the British in control of Philadelphia while Washington's army was camped several miles away at Valley Forge. The British maintained sizeable garrisons at New York and Newport, and despite the surrender of Burgoyne's army, Canada was still protected by a large garrison.

While the main American army began the year several miles from Philadelphia at Valley Forge, there were substantial detachments at Wilmington, Delaware and Albany, New York. American forces also held the important southern cities of Savannah and Charleston.

While the British government and George III remained steadfast in their support of the war, Burgoyne's surrender at Saratoga led to a reassessment of British military strategy. Burgoyne's surrender buoyed American hopes of direct French intervention. Concerned that the British appeared willing to make concessions to the American colonists, France proposed expanded assistance and in January a treaty of commerce and military alliance was agreed upon and signed in early February. Rather than an immediate declaration of war, the agreement gave France discretion as to when they would open hostilities. At the same time, they approached Spain with a proposal to enter a military alliance, which was rejected.

In response to Burgoyne's surrender and the prospect of an American alliance with France, the British government proposed a dramatic shift in policy. The proposal stopped short of recognising American independence but recognised the rights of the American colonists and included expanded specific safeguards. In early April a peace commission, headed by the Earl of Carlisle, sailed for America carrying the British proposal.

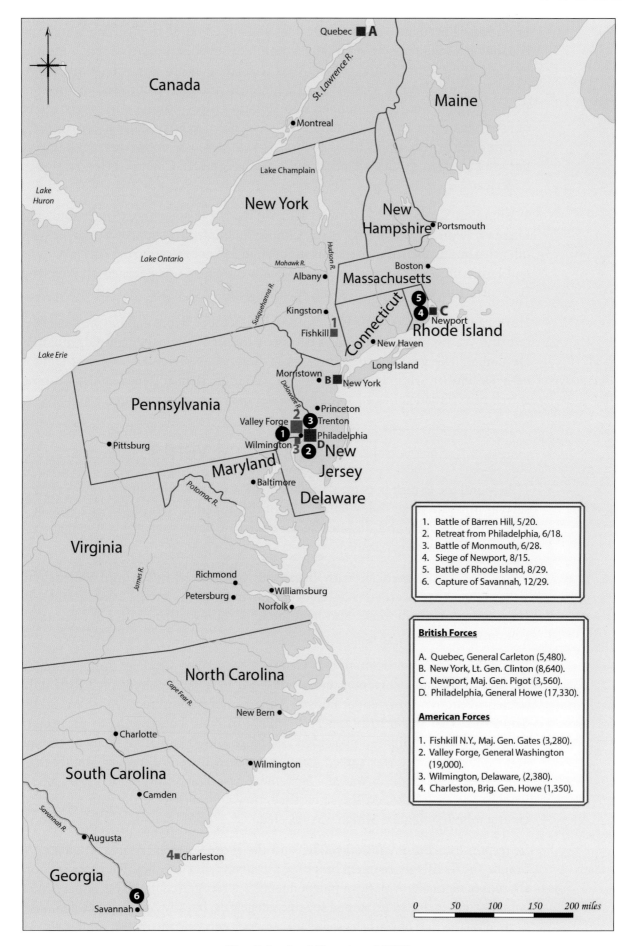

Quebec ■A

Canada

Maine

Montreal

Lake Champlain

Lake
Huron

New York

New
Hampshire ● Portsmouth

Lake Ontario

Mohawk R.

Albany ●   Boston ●

Massachusetts

Kingston ●

Fishkill ■ **1**   ● New Haven

Connecticut

Rhode Island

Newport

5
4 ■ C

Long Island

Lake Erie

Morristown
● B ■
● New York

Pennsylvania

● Princeton
2 ■ **3** ● Trenton
Valley Forge
1 ■ ● Philadelphia
Wilmington ■ **3**
2 ● D **New**
Jersey

● Pittsburg

Maryland

● Baltimore

Delaware

Potomac R.

Virginia

James R.

Richmond ●
● Williamsburg
Petersburg ●
Norfolk ●

1. Battle of Barren Hill, 5/20.
2. Retreat from Philadelphia, 6/18.
3. Battle of Monmouth, 6/28.
4. Siege of Newport, 8/15.
5. Battle of Rhode Island, 8/29.
6. Capture of Savannah, 12/29.

North Carolina

Cape Fear R.

New Bern ●

British Forces

A. Quebec, General Carleton (5,480).
B. New York, Lt. Gen. Clinton (8,640).
C. Newport, Maj. Gen. Pigot (3,560).
D. Philadelphia, General Howe (17,330).

● Charlotte

South Carolina

● Wilmington

● Camden

American Forces

1. Fishkill N.Y., Maj. Gen. Gates (3,280).
2. Valley Forge, General Washington
   (19,000).
3. Wilmington, Delaware, (2,380).
4. Charleston, Brig. Gen. Howe (1,350).

Savannah R.

● Augusta

4 ■ Charleston

Georgia

6

Savannah ●

0   50   100   150   200 miles

The Principal Events of 1778

With the resignation of General Howe in late 1777, General Clinton was appointed overall commander-in-chief. Along with Clinton's appointment, the British government adopted a revised military strategy that recognised while a complete military victory was not probable, American independence could be prevented. Uppermost in the British calculation was that war with France, and possibly Spain would require a shift in military resources to protect their possessions in the West Indies. The strategy proposed transferring a major portion of British naval resources and 10,000 troops from the colonies to the West Indies and Canada.

The strategy also recognised the New England colonies were largely irreconcilable, but that Loyalist sentiment was most pronounced in the southern colonies and to a more limited degree in the middle colonies. By protecting Canada and the West Indies and maintaining a strong presence in the southern colonies, the British could retain a powerful position in North America and limit American expansion. From these discussions was conceived the 'Southern Strategy' which would guide military operations in 1778 and beyond.

During the Spring of 1778 minor skirmishes continued around Philadelphia and in New Jersey as both sides attempted to gather supplies from the surrounding countryside. Clinton attempted to cut off Major General Lafayette from Barren Hill on 20 May, but the Americans were able to retreat. As a result of the directives from London, Clinton evacuated Philadelphia on 16 June, sending a portion of his forces by ship but marching the bulk of his army across New Jersey, followed by Washington's Continentals and growing numbers of American militia. The inconclusive battle of Monmouth on 28 June allowed Clinton to continue his withdrawal to New York. In July, a combined force of Loyalists and Native Americans launched an offensive in the Wyoming Valley, capturing militia outposts and denying the resources to Washington's army.

In late July, a French fleet commanded by *Vice-Amiral* Count d'Estaing arrived off the New Jersey coast with 16 ships and 4,000 men. The French were too late to intercept the British fleet evacuating Philadelphia and disappointed that the channel at New York was too shallow to allow safe passage to support an attack on New York City. Washington and d'Estaing shifted their focus to a joint Franco-American attack. D'Estaing's fleet arrived off Rhode Island on 28 July and Sullivan advanced to Providence on 15 August, but on 20 August the French announced they were withdrawing their fleet due to damage caused by a massive storm and inconclusive naval engagements with the British fleet. Sullivan withdrew and evacuated before the arrival of Clinton with a relief force.

In December, Clinton dispatched 3,500 troops under the command of Colonel Campbell to Savannah, Georgia. The convoy arrived on 23 December and quickly captured the city on 29 December.

1779 Strategic Events

1779 found both General Washington and General Clinton facing reductions in their manpower and so were reduced to having limited options as the new campaign began. Although the capture of Savannah in December 1778 established a British foothold in the southern colonies consistent with a broader strategy of shifting the main focus of the war to the south; maintaining this foothold would require additional resources. In

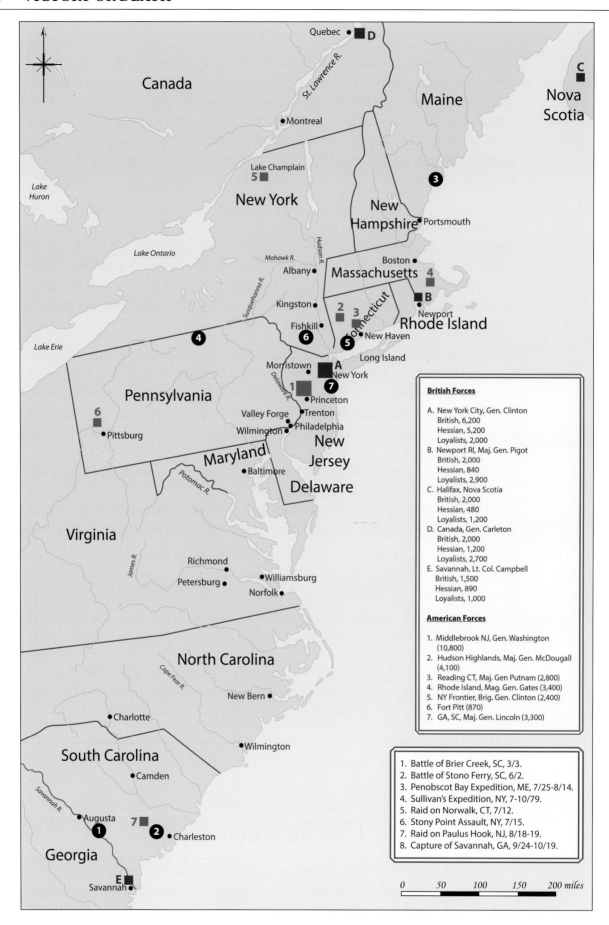

British Forces

A. New York City, Gen. Clinton
British, 6,200
Hessian, 5,200
Loyalists, 2,000
B. Newport RI, Maj. Gen. Pigot
British, 2,000
Hessian, 840
Loyalists, 2,900
C. Halifax, Nova Scotia
British, 2,000
Hessian, 480
Loyalists, 1,200
D. Canada, Gen. Carleton
British, 2,000
Hessian, 1,200
Loyalists, 2,700
E. Savannah, Lt. Col. Campbell
British, 1,500
Hessian, 890
Loyalists, 1,000

American Forces

1. Middlebrook NJ, Gen. Washington (10,800)
2. Hudson Highlands, Maj. Gen. McDougall (4,100)
3. Reading CT, Maj. Gen Putnam (2,800)
4. Rhode Island, Mag. Gen. Gates (3,400)
5. NY Frontier, Brig. Gen. Clinton (2,400)
6. Fort Pitt (870)
7. GA, SC, Maj. Gen. Lincoln (3,300)

1. Battle of Brier Creek, SC, 3/3.
2. Battle of Stono Ferry, SC, 6/2.
3. Penobscot Bay Expedition, ME, 7/25-8/14.
4. Sullivan's Expedition, NY, 7-10/79.
5. Raid on Norwalk, CT, 7/12.
6. Stony Point Assault, NY, 7/15.
7. Raid on Paulus Hook, NJ, 8/18-19.
8. Capture of Savannah, GA, 9/24-10/19.

The Principal Events of 1779

addition to detaching troops to the south, Clinton was also required to send veteran units of his army to the West Indies to meet the anticipated French threat. In exchange, Clinton was sent recently trained replacements untested in combat. While the bulk of the British forces were concentrated in New York, garrisons also held Newport and Quebec and a sizeable force was located in Newfoundland.

Similarly, the British offensive in the southern colonies required General Washington to further dilute his main army by detaching veteran Continental units. Washington remained in winter quarters in Middlebrook, New Jersey and maintained detachments in the Hudson Highlands, Connecticut and Rhode Island. The British alliance with Native American tribes required the allocation of troops on the New York frontier and Major General Lincoln collected a larger garrison at Charleston in the face of a renewed British threat.

On the heels of the fallout from the failed attack on Rhode Island, Washington was forced to address Congressional interest in organising an invasion of Canada, in conjunction with the French. Although the French had no interest in recapturing Canada, Congressional interest increased throughout 1779, culminating in a plan, drawn up by a Congressional committee, that was presented to Washington. Recognising that the French would not support a Canadian invasion, Washington responded to Congress pointing out various shortcomings of the proposed plan and it was quietly dropped.

During the course of the year, the French successfully negotiated an alliance with the Spanish, hoping to threaten an invasion of Britain, while holding out the prospect of a return of Gibraltar to Spain

In January, Brigadier General Augustine Prevost assumed command of the British troops at Savannah and dispatched Lieutenant Colonel Campbell into the Georgia backcountry to capture Augusta, Georgia and raise Loyalist units. The British defeated American forces at Brier Creek on 3 March and consolidated their control of Savannah and Georgia.

In the spring, American and British forces, assisted by Loyalist and militia units, manoeuvred through South Carolina and Georgia attempting to gain a strategic advantage. Major General Lincoln marched from Charleston towards Augusta. In late April, Lincoln assembled a large force of militia to supplement recent reinforcements and marched from Charleston towards Augusta after leaving behind a small force of militia. Brigadier General Prevost learned of Lincoln's movement and drove Brigadier General Moultrie back to Charleston. Alerted to Prevost's advance Lincoln reversed course to return to Charleston, but Prevost was informed of Lincoln's return and retreated towards Savannah, leaving a rearguard at Stono Ferry, which Lincoln attacked on 20 June.

In July, Washington directed Major General John Sullivan to undertake an extended campaign against the Iroquois Confederation on the western frontier. Clinton organised a series of coastal raids to capture or destroy American supplies and disrupt privateers operating from those bases. British forces raided Newport, Virginia in May, followed by attacks on New Haven and Norwalk, Connecticut. In June, the British captured Penobscot Bay in the Maine territory, an act intended to protect British shipping and secure timber resources.

From the start of the war, American control of the Hudson Highlands was critical to maintaining communications and supplies from New England to the lower colonies. In June, Clinton led an expedition that captured the strategic King's Crossing between Stony Point and Verplank's Point on the Hudson River. Clinton's action also threatened the American fortress at West Point and in response, Washington ordered an assault on the British fortifications at Stony Point on 15 July. The attack was successful and followed by a similar attack on the British garrison at Paulus Hook on 19 August.

1780 Strategic Events

In deciding to embark a large portion of the British forces in New York City for an attack on Charleston South Carolina, Clinton chose to abandon the defence of Newport Rhode, Island and transfer those troops to New York. That left small garrisons to protect Quebec, Halifax and Penobscott. German *Generalleiutenant* von Knyphausen was left to command the New York garrison. Clinton sailed to Savannah where he paused before advancing towards Charleston.

Washington and the main Continental army remained at Morristown, with troops continuing to safeguard the Hudson Highlands and detachments protecting the western frontier. Several brigades of Continental troops were in Virginia on their way to Charleston.

After a difficult voyage south, Clinton sailed north from Savannah and landed on Saint Johns Island on 11 February. Clinton paused for several weeks to allow for the arrival of additional troops from New York, which allowed reinforcements to bolster the defence of Charleston. After slowly tightening the ring around Charleston in April, he completed the encirclement with the capture of Monck's Corner on 14 April. On 12 May, after a siege of 44 days, Charleston surrendered. Clinton then dispatched columns to secure the South Carolina back country. British troops scattered the American militia, many of whom accepted the terms of parole offered by Clinton and returned home. Lieutenant Colonel Tarleton destroyed a column of Virginia Continentals at Waxhaws on 29 June.

Believing South Carolina secured, Clinton appointed Lieutenant General Cornwallis overall commander at Charleston, commanding 3,000 men, before returning with the bulk of his troops to New York City.

As Clinton was consolidating control over South Carolina, von Knyphausen prepared to invade New Jersey, unaware that Clinton planned a similar action once he had returned to New York.

In June, von Knyphausen marched from New York into New Jersey, fighting actions at Connecticut Farms on 7 June and Springfield on 23 June before retiring.

In July, *Lieutenant Général* Comte de Rochambeau arrived in Newport with 5,000 French soldiers and a naval squadron.

In the aftermath of the Charleston debacle, Congress appointed Major General Gates to command the Southern Department and after collecting reinforcements from Washington, marched south to confront Cornwallis. A preliminary skirmish at Hanging Rock on 5 August was followed by a disastrous American defeat at Camden on 16 August.

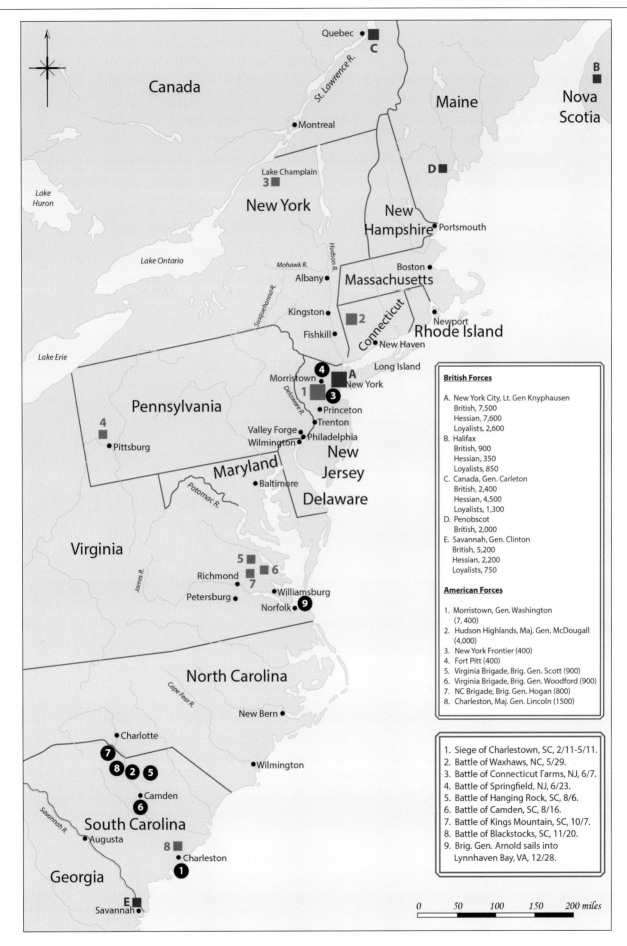

British Forces

A. New York City, Lt. Gen Knyphausen
   British, 7,500
   Hessian, 7,600
   Loyalists, 2,600
B. Halifax
   British, 900
   Hessian, 350
   Loyalists, 850
C. Canada, Gen. Carleton
   British, 2,400
   Hessian, 4,500
   Loyalists, 1,300
D. Penobscot
   British, 2,000
E. Savannah, Gen. Clinton
   British, 5,200
   Hessian, 2,200
   Loyalists, 750

American Forces

1. Morristown, Gen. Washington
   (7, 400)
2. Hudson Highlands, Maj. Gen. McDougall
   (4,000)
3. New York Frontier (400)
4. Fort Pitt (400)
5. Virginia Brigade, Brig. Gen. Scott (900)
6. Virginia Brigade, Brig. Gen. Woodford (900)
7. NC Brigade, Brig. Gen. Hogan (800)
8. Charleston, Maj. Gen. Lincoln (1500)

1. Siege of Charlestown, SC, 2/11-5/11.
2. Battle of Waxhaws, NC, 5/29.
3. Battle of Connecticut Farms, NJ, 6/7.
4. Battle of Springfield, NJ, 6/23.
5. Battle of Hanging Rock, SC, 8/6.
6. Battle of Camden, SC, 8/16.
7. Battle of Kings Mountain, SC, 10/7.
8. Battle of Blackstocks, SC, 11/20.
9. Brig. Gen. Arnold sails into
   Lynnhaven Bay, VA, 12/28.

The Strategic Events of 1780

While Cornwallis consolidated British control over the Carolina coast and backcountry, Major General Nathanael Greene was sent south to take command of the remnants of the American army. The victories at Charleston and Camden bolstered Loyalist sentiment allowing Lieutenant Colonel Patrick Ferguson to organise a large Loyalist force. Ferguson issued a challenge to the frontier mountain settlements in North Carolina, demanding that they declare loyalty to the Crown or face destruction. In response, a large force of American militia marched against Ferguson, destroying his command at King's Mountain on 7 October.

Cornwallis ordered Lieutenant Colonel Banestare Tarleton to counter the growing strength of the American militia. Tarleton fought an action at Blackstocks on 20 November that ended inconclusively.

Responding to a request from Cornwallis for a diversionary expedition to Virginia, in December Clinton dispatched Brigadier General Benedict Arnold with 1,600 men to raid American supply depots and disrupt shipping.

1781 Strategic Events

At the beginning of 1781 General Clinton remained around New York where his troops were facing American detachments holding the Hudson Highlands

Rochambeau was camped at Newport, Rhode Island, while British garrisons at Quebec and Penobscot remained in place.

The primary focus of military activity was now the southern colonies. Lieutenant General Cornwallis began the year at Charlotte, North Carolina, while Brigadier General Arnold, prepared to move along the James River from Norfolk to Richmond. British garrisons were scattered at small forts across South Carolina and Georgia. Faced with Cornwallis' overwhelming strength, Major General Greene split his forces, retiring into North Carolina while dispatching Brigadier General Morgan to western South Carolina.

The reverses in South Carolina and the stalemate in the north, coupled with a continuing economic crisis and fear that the lack of success might result in withdrawal of French support, caused many to fear the collapse of the American effort.

In January, elements of the Pennsylvania Line mutinied due to lack of pay and miserable living conditions. Although Major General Wayne, dispatched by Washington to address their grievances was successful, the New Jersey Line followed suit and also mutinied. Major General Robert Howe disarmed the rebellious soldiers and arrested the ringleaders, who were tried and executed, ending the crisis.

In March, France approved another large loan, which was necessary to keep the American war effort alive.

Cornwallis reacted to Greene's detaching of Morgan to western South Carolina by ordering Lieutenant Colonel Tarleton to find and destroy him. Tarleton found Morgan at Cowpens and suffered a defeat on 17 January. During January and February, Cornwallis pursued Greene across North Carolina without success until the Americans gave battle at Guildford Courthouse on 15 March. Cornwallis retired to Wilmington,

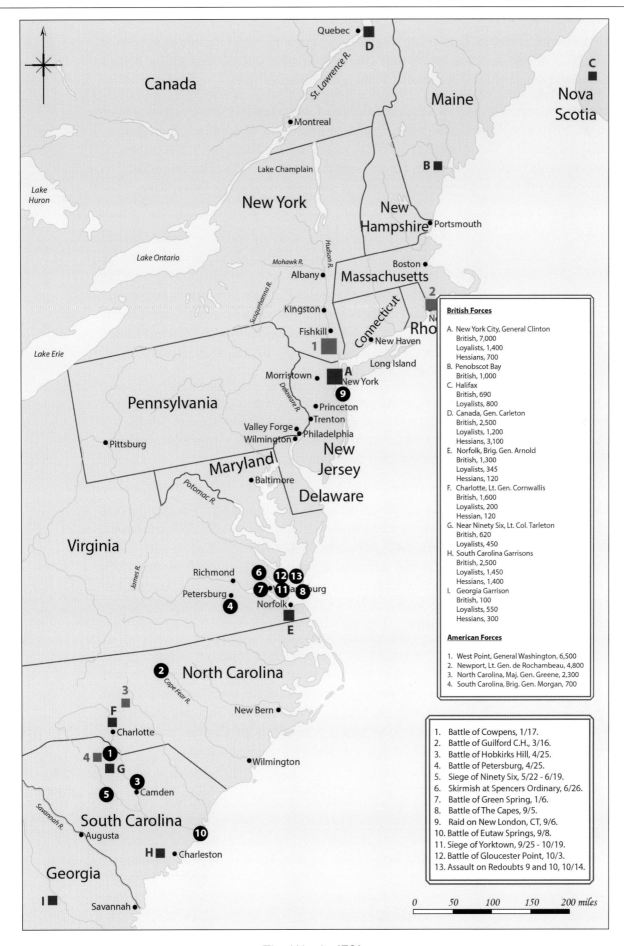

The War in 1781

British Forces

A. New York City, General Clinton
   British, 7,000
   Loyalists, 1,400
   Hessians, 700
B. Penobscot Bay
   British, 1,000
C. Halifax
   British, 690
   Loyalists, 800
D. Canada, Gen. Carleton
   British, 2,500
   Loyalists, 1,200
   Hessians, 3,100
E. Norfolk, Brig. Gen. Arnold
   British, 1,300
   Loyalists, 345
   Hessians, 120
F. Charlotte, Lt. Gen. Cornwallis
   British, 1,600
   Loyalists, 200
   Hessian, 120
G. Near Ninety Six, Lt. Col. Tarleton
   British, 620
   Loyalists, 450
H. South Carolina Garrisons
   British, 2,500
   Loyalists, 1,450
   Hessians, 1,400
I. Georgia Garrison
   British, 100
   Loyalists, 550
   Hessians, 300

American Forces

1. West Point, General Washington, 6,500
2. Newport, Lt. Gen. de Rochambeau, 4,800
3. North Carolina, Maj. Gen. Greene, 2,300
4. South Carolina, Brig. Gen. Morgan, 700

1. Battle of Cowpens, 1/17.
2. Battle of Guilford C.H., 3/16.
3. Battle of Hobkirks Hill, 4/25.
4. Battle of Petersburg, 4/25.
5. Siege of Ninety Six, 5/22 - 6/19.
6. Skirmish at Spencers Ordinary, 6/26.
7. Battle of Green Spring, 1/6.
8. Battle of The Capes, 9/5.
9. Raid on New London, CT, 9/6.
10. Battle of Eutaw Springs, 9/8.
11. Siege of Yorktown, 9/25 - 10/19.
12. Battle of Gloucester Point, 10/3.
13. Assault on Redoubts 9 and 10, 10/14.

North Carolina (briefly), before moving into Virginia in May. Rather than follow Cornwallis, Greene marched into South Carolina to confront the remaining British garrisons and defeated Lord Rawdon at Hobkirk's Hill on 25 April.

In Virginia, British Brigadier General Arnold struck out from Norfolk along the James River, destroying privateers and capturing large quantities of supplies. In response, Washington ordered Major General Lafayette south in February, with 1,200 troops, to buttress Virginia's defences. A small French squadron also sailed to Hampton Road to confront Arnold's fleet but lacking the ability to sail into the shallow James River, they withdrew.

In March, Washington travelled to Newport to discuss strategy with *Lieutenant Général* Comte de Rochambeau. They agreed to send a larger French fleet, accompanied by 1,200 soldiers, to Virginia to support Lafayette. At the same time Clinton, alarmed by news of French activity, dispatched Major General Phillips to Virginia to support Arnold. The French fleet was defeated by British warships on 16 March at Cape Henry, forcing the French to return to Newport while Phillips landed on 26 March. Phillips and Arnold marched inland, destroying American supply depots at Petersburg on 25 April and Richmond, and scattering the Virginia militia.

As Cornwallis moved into Virginia, Major General Greene continued to struggle against British strongholds in South Carolina, failing to take the village of Ninety Six after a siege that lasted from 22 May to 18 June. Greene fought another inconclusive battle in Eutaw Springs, South Carolina, on 8 September.

Cornwallis ordered Phillips to meet him at Petersburg, but Phillips died of fever on 15 May before Cornwallis arrived on 20 May. Cornwallis continued his raids throughout Virginia during the whole of June before retiring towards his base at Norfolk, shadowed much of the time by Lafayette who was joined by Major General Wayne with 1,200 Pennsylvania Continentals. Lafayette harassed Cornwallis' rearguard at Spencer's Ordinary on 26 June and skirmished with the British as they crossed the James River at Green Spring on 6 July. Acting on orders from Clinton, Cornwallis sought a place to establish a port and chose Yorktown.

Washington and Rochambeau continued to evaluate their options, assessing the defences at New York. Washington was committed to an attack on New York City and its outlying forts, but a thorough reconnaissance determined the fortifications were too strong for a direct attack. By early August, with an attack on New York not viable and news that a French fleet was sailing to confront the British in the Chesapeake Bay, the decision was made to march both the American and French armies south.

The Royal Navy was defeated on 5 September off the Virginia coast at the Battle of the Capes and returned to New York for repairs. Arnold, recently returned from Virginia, organised a raid on New London, Connecticut on 6 September, hoping to delay the movement of the combined French and American army. The combined American and French army marched south and opened the siege of Yorktown on 28 September. Clinton organised a sizeable relief force in New York in early October but had difficulty in assembling adequate transports and warships delayed the sailing until 19 October. On that day Cornwallis formally surrendered.

After capturing the island of Grenada in July, *Vice-Amiral* d'Estaing sailed north to attack Savannah in collaboration with Major General Lincoln in Charleston. D'Estaing laid siege to the city after calling for its surrender while the British attempted to reinforce the garrison. Concerned about the hurricane threat to his fleet, d'Estaing and Lincoln agreed to assault the British defences on 9 October. The joint assault failed and after d'Estaing sailed south to the West Indies, Major General Lincoln retired to Charleston. In December, Clinton embarked from New York City, sailing south to capture Charleston.

1782 Strategic Events

The surrender of Cornwallis at Yorktown in October 1781 did not end hostilities between the Americans and British but did change the intensity of the struggle and focus of the war.

Colonial Secretary Lord George Germain received word of Cornwallis' surrender on 25 November. Parliament convened on 27 November and received an address from George III, expressing his desire to continue the war in America. After several weeks of debate, on 12 December Parliament voted on a minority resolution proposing to end the war. Although the resolution was defeated, the King rejected Lord North's request to resign and Parliament recessed on 20 December, without resolving how best to proceed.

Clinton and Graves returned to New York on 7 November where Cornwallis, who returned to New York in early November, refused to meet with Clinton and joined a convoy headed for England on 15 November.

Clinton resigned in January 1782, followed by Lord Germain in February. Clinton was replaced by Sir Guy Carleton who arrived in New York on 5 May. Carleton found the garrison at New York amounted to 18,000 British and German troops but the garrisons at Charleston and Savanah were woefully understrength.

Despite British weakness in the south, American Major General Greene, joined by Major General Wayne, made limited headway in forcing the enemy to retreat to Charleston or Savannah due to continuing infighting and disagreements between civil and military authorities, and the difficulty in organising adequate militia forces to supplement the small core of Continentals.

In May, Carleton directed Major General Alexander Leslie, overall commander of British forces in the south, to withdraw the garrisons from both Savannah and Saint Augustine, Florida, before abandoning Charleston to return to New York. Savannah was fully evacuated by the end of July, but a lack of transports delayed the withdrawal from Charleston until December.

Although Parliament maintained previous levels of military spending, they stipulated an end to the policy of 'offensive' actions from the remaining strongholds in the former colonies, effectively ending hostilities in America. With the struggle in North America over, British resources were focused on defending their possessions in the West Indies.

As Parliament debated British military strategy through the spring of 1782, the Prime Minister, Lord North, was replaced in March by the Marquis of Rockingham. With news of more reverses in the West Indies and the loss of Minorca in the Mediterranean, the new British administration opened negotiations with the American government.

Throughout the remainder of 1782, a complicated process of negotiations took place between Britain, the United States, France and Spain. The 1778 Treaty of Alliance between the United States and France stipulated no peace treaty could be signed without the approval of France. At the same time, France's agreement with Spain required Spanish approval of any treaty between the French and the British. Spain was insistent that the French assist them in the recapture of Gibraltar before the war ended. Although an ally of France, Spain had no treaty with the United States and openly advocated against their interests.

When American negotiators became aware of a French proposal to limit the American territorial boundaries to an area east of the Appalachian Mountains, they opened direct contact with the British. Hoping to split the Americans from their French allies, the British agreed to more generous terms. A host of other issues were also addressed including fishing rights off Newfoundland and in the Gulf of Mexico, as well as establishing the Mississippi River as the western boundary of the United States. With the failure of the Franco-Spanish assault on Gibraltar, the French accepted the preliminary peace treaty between Great Britain and the United States of America on 30 November 1782.

A more expansive treaty was signed on 20 January 1783, which largely returned British and French possessions to their original pre-war owners in the West Indies. The Spanish retained Minorca and added West Florida to their East Florida possessions, although the northern boundary with the United States was not clarified until 1795. The British agreed to recognise the Canadian boundary with the United States as reflected in the 1763 treaty with France rather than the Quebec Act of 1774. The agreement granted the United States the Northwest Territory, a large area east of the Mississippi River and north of the Ohio River that would eventually evolve into five new states.

The final peace treaty between the United States and Great Britain was signed on 3 September 1783.

3

West Indies

By the mid eighteenth century, British, French, Dutch and Spanish possessions scattered throughout the West Indies had become vitally important as major generators of revenue through the production of sugar and other natural resources. While restoring control over the rebellious 13 colonies was the primary focus of British military strategy, as it became clear that France and Spain might enter the war on the side of the Americans, attention turned to protecting and expanding British holdings in the West Indies.

Although American forces successfully raided Nassau in the Bahamas in March 1776, the limited naval resources available to the Americans restricted further actions to attacks on British shipping by privateers rather than any further direct threats to their island possessions.

All that changed in 1778 with the entry of France, followed by Spain in early 1780, into the war as allies of the Americans. On 7 September, French forces invaded and captured Dominica. The British response was to invade Saint Lucia on 15 December and defeat a French relief force under *Contre-Amiral* d'Estaing, capturing the island on 28 December.

After both sides reinforced their naval and land forces in early 1779, the French, informed that the British fleet was accompanying a large convoy from Saint Kitts, took the opportunity to capture Saint Vincent on 18 June, followed by Grenada on 4 July; defeating a British relief force on 6 July. 1779 ended with the British defeat of a French naval force on 18 December near Martinique.

In early 1780, Admiral Sir George Rodney arrived at Barbados from a command in the Mediterranean, while French *Contre-Amiral* de Guichen took command in Martinique. In April, de Guichen embarked 3,000 troops, intending to assault British possessions after providing security for a convoy sailing for Santo Domingo. Rodney, informed of the French movement, sailed, intercepting and defeating de Guichen in the channel between Martinique and Dominica on 17 April. De Guichon retired to Guadeloupe and after refitting, sailed again towards Saint Lucia. Rodney intercepted the French again and after almost two weeks of manoeuvring the fleets, fought a series of actions resulting in a French defeat.

Intelligence reached Rodney at Barbados that a large Spanish fleet had sailed in late April for the West Indies. The British fleet was deployed east of Martinique but the

Spanish, joined by de Guichen, avoided the British and anchored in Martinique. Despite the unwillingness of the Spanish to undertake joint operations, de Guichen accompanied the Spanish to Havana in July, before sailing back to Cadiz in August. At the same time, learning of the French movements and alerted to the beginning of the hurricane season, Rodney sailed to New York, before returning to the West Indies in early December.

Major hurricanes in 1780 decimated most of the islands, destroying port and supply facilities and damaging or sinking warships and transports. Rodney, falsely informed that the French defences at Saint Vincent had been destroyed, landed troops on the island on 15 December but finding the French defences intact re-embarked and returned to Saint Lucia, where he was joined by reinforcements commanded by Rear Admiral Hood in January 1781.

Rodney received a dispatch on 27 January announcing a declaration of war with The Netherlands, ordering him to capture the islands of Saint Eustatius and Saint Martin. Saint Eustatius was a major port, which had become a major conduit for supplies of arms, powder and other materiel to the Americans.

On 3 February, Rodney compelled Saint Eustatius to surrender, along with Saint Martin and Saba. While Rodney spent the next three months cataloguing the immense booty captured at Saint Eustatius, Hood was dispatched to first intercept a French convoy, which proved illusionary and then proceeded to blockade Fort Royal, Martinique. A large French convoy, commanded by *Contre-Amiral* de Grasse did sail from France at the end of March. The French fleet was sighted on 28 April and the fleets engaged indecisively on 29 April, although Hood retired the next day and rejoined Rodney on 11 May.

After a failed attempt to retake Saint Lucia, on 10 May de Grasse dispatched a task force of ships and troops to attack Tobago. Rodney responded by sending a small fleet under Admiral Drake on 29 May. After finding a large French fleet at Tobago, Drake retired to wait for Rodney to arrive, which he did on 4 June, only to discover the British garrison had surrendered on 2 June. De Grasse retired to Martinique while Rodney and Hood returned to Barbados. De Grasse sailed on 5 July bound for Haiti, before proceeding to Virginia to support the encirclement of Cornwallis at Yorktown.

After being reinforced in early 1782 at Saint Kitts, Hood awaited the arrival of Rodney with additional ships. While the French primary objective for 1782 was the capture of Jamaica, de Grasse attempted to attack Barbados, but contrary winds and currents frustrated his progress, and he focused his attention on Saint Kitts. The French fleet arrived off Saint Kitts on 11 January, forcing the British garrison to retire to the fort at Brimstone Hill. Hood responded to news of the French arrival on 14 January and sailed to Antigua for minor repairs before embarking additional troops and arrived off Saint Kitts on 23 January. After several days of manoeuvring off the coast, the two fleets clashed on 25 January and into the early hours of 26 January. Although the British fleet outmanoeuvred de Grasse, anchored in the protection of the harbour, Hood was unable to rescue the garrison, which surrendered on 13 February. The islands of Nevis and Montserrat were also lost to the French, although Hood made good his escape from Frigate Bay.

Hood was joined by Rodney on 25 February, but their combined fleet was unable to intercept de Grasse before he returned to Martinique. To protect against the anticipated strike at Jamaica, Rodney deployed his fleet between Dominica and Martinique, failing to intercept a large supply convoy that brought reinforcements to de Grasse. De Grasse sailed on 8 April hoping to ferry his large fleet of transports around the edge of the British fleet, but Rodney, immediately informed of the French departure, issued from Saint Lucia and spotted the French early on 9 April. De Grasse responded by detaching a portion of his warships to attack the British. After an inconclusive skirmish that afternoon, the British continued their pursuit over the next several days, and on 12 April the Battle of The Saints ended in a decisive British victory and the capture of de Grasse. British pursuit of the scattered French fleet further frustrated de Grasse's plans to invade Jamaica. Rodney was relieved on 10 July by Admiral Pigot, who ordered the fleet to New York, where they remained until October before returning to the Caribbean.

Although the French and Spanish assembled an armada of over 66 warships and 24,000 men at Cadiz, intended to resume an offensive in the West Indies in early January 1783, the signing of a peace treaty on 20 January brought an end to hostilities and the disbanding of the fleet.

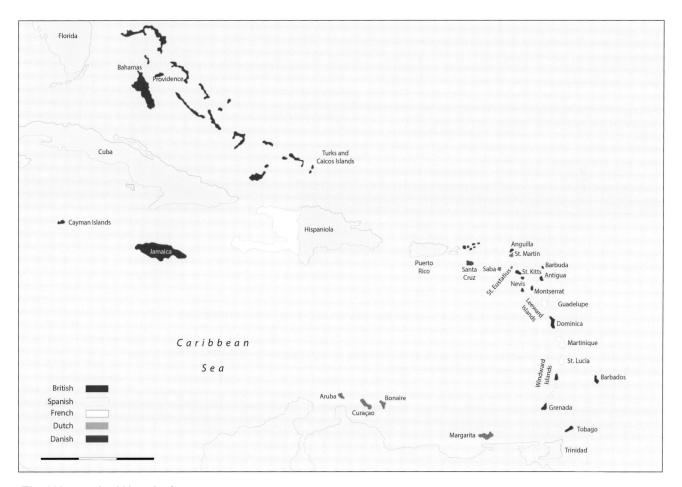

The War in the West Indies

4

The Armies of the American Revolution

The following sections are intended to provide an overview of the organisation of the armies that fought in the Revolution, documenting the evolution of their structure throughout the course of the war. While the British and German organisation varied somewhat through the war, the size, composition and organisational structure of American regiments varied to a much greater degree, particularly during the early years of the war. In building units intended to refight the battles of the Revolutionary War an understanding of the organisation and training of each belligerent is important. This section also includes a summary of the tactical doctrine that guided the training of the officer corps for the Americans and British.

While we recognise that Loyalists serving in the British army were 'Americans' in the same sense as Continental or militia soldiers, for purposes of clarity this guide will refer to those troops supporting the rebellion as American. When the war began the fundamental governmental organisation in America was an individual colony. At the time of the Declaration of Independence in July 1776 the phrase 'United Colonies' was used but in September 1776 the Continental Congress adopted a resolution to replace that term with the United States of America. As the war progressed the Continental Congress assumed greater responsibility for governing the conduct of the war. For this guide, the reference to either colony or state is interchangeable, there being no discernible difference between the two.

For wargaming the American Revolution, the regiment is the basic combat formation, although some skirmish rules systems allow for the use of companies as manoeuvre units. Artillery units are usually represented by sections, composed of two guns, attached to brigades or organised into artillery reserves. The cavalry was also organised into regiments, composed of squadrons and troops. Many battles of the period included one or two individual squadrons, which tended to operate as independent units. It was rare for complete cavalry regiments to manoeuvre as a single unit.

For the purposes of this book, references to battalions and regiments in most cases are interchangeable. British and American regiments were normally composed of one battalion. In the opening months of the war many American militia and some Continental units were referred to as battalions but as a practical matter their organisation and size did not vary significantly from regiments. During those early years, the number of companies making up a regiment and the strength of individual companies varied widely for the Americans. Each colony structured their companies and regiments somewhat differently. At the urging of General George Washington, the Continental Congress adopted a scheme in late 1775 to standardise the structure of the Continental units to be raised by each colony. While over time most Continental regiments were similarly organised, state regiments and militia formations continued to adopt different structures. Over the course of the war the organisation of the American army was modified to adapt to the nature of the war.

Comparatively, the organisation of British and German regiments was more standardised, as was the structure of Loyalist and Provincial units.

American Organisation and Training

American Militia

Throughout the seven years struggle the American army was composed of a range of Continental regiments, State regiments and militia units. With the outbreak of open hostilities between American and British forces in April 1775 American militia composed the bulk of the revolutionary forces.

The growth and development of the 13 colonies in North America included not just the expansion of settlements but the development of militia in the colonies. This militia, beginning in 1611 in Virginia, grew in size and responsibility to protect those colonies

Early war American militia unit illustrating the variety of dress. Old Glory and Wargames Foundry 28mm figures.

from attacks from Native American tribes and incursions from European powers bent of acquiring more holdings in North America. Eventually every colony except for Pennsylvania enacted laws to create a militia.

The evolution of the militia system reached maturity during the French and Indian War, which largely set the stage for the role of militia with the beginning of hostilities with Britain in 1775.

Militia laws required the enrolment of all free males between the ages of 16 and 50. These men were organised into companies and regiments commanded by officers appointed by the Governor. In 1774 Connecticut enrolled 26,000 militiamen while in 1775 New Jersey organised 26 regiments of infantry and 11 troops of horse, and Pennsylvania created 53 battalions of infantry.

1775

In early April 1775, the Provincial Congress sent representatives to surrounding colonies to request military assistance. The militia from these colonies were organised in a similar manner to that of Massachusetts. All these militias responded to the increasing tension between the colonies and Britain by securing weapons, powder and ammunition. The British responded by conducting raids on militia supply bases. The failed raid against Concord and Lexington in April 1775 brought events to a head.

In the aftermath of Lexington and Concord the Congress adopted a plan that called for a New England army of 30,000 men, with Massachusetts contributing 13,600. The Continental Congress resolved that the militia should bring with them a firelock musket, bayonet, sword or bayonet, 24 rounds in a cartridge box, a powder horn and knapsack.

In June 1775, the Continental Congress adopted three resolutions. The first was to assume control and responsibility for the forces, largely composed of New England troops, gathered around Boston thereby establishing the Continental Army. In addition, George Washington was appointed General and Commander-in-Chief of the Continental Army and finally adopted a code of rules and regulations for the

American militia units advancing. 28mm Dixon, Old Glory and Wargames Foundry figures. The units are armed with a mix of muskets and rifles.

governance of the army. At that time troops from Massachusetts represented most of the army, joined by men from New Hampshire, Connecticut and Rhode Island. Over the next several months units from New York, Pennsylvania and Virgina joined the army.

While the specific organisation of militia battalions or regiments varied, the basic structures were similar from colony to colony. The core of militia regiments were the musket or rifle companies, led in most cases by a captain. The command structure included a lieutenant, an ensign and several sergeants. A drummer and fifer rounded out individual companies. Each regiment also included a small headquarters group composed of a colonel, lieutenant colonel, major, quartermaster and staff, a surgeon and an armourer. The regiments were named after their colonels in most cases.

Massachusetts

In October 1774, the new Massachusetts Provincial Congress reorganised the militia, requiring each company to re-elect officers, and those officers elected new regimental or battalion commanders.

The Massachusetts militia was organised on a geographic basis with each county being required to raise a regiment. The size of each regiment, which was more often an administrative structure rather than a tactical formation, was based on the relative population of the county, composed of companies from each village or town. Company officers were elected by the company while regimental officers were appointed by the Governor.

The militia was also divided into three distinct formations. Anywhere from one-quarter to one-third of the militia were designated as 'Minutemen;' companies intended to be able to muster on a minutes' notice. These companies, composed of up to 64 men, were to be trained using the British 1764 Drill Manual and were grouped with other similar companies to form special regiments of 10 companies. The bulk of militia companies were organised as before, varying in size based on local population, but organised into regiments of 6 to 15 companies. Alarm companies were composed of men too old or young to serve in the regular militia companies and were expected to be the last line of defence.

Massachusetts militia regiment, 28mm Old Glory figures. As the siege of Boston continued in 1775 American militia units grew larger but there was no uniformity of dress.

Massachusetts organised 23 infantry regiments and one artillery regiment into the 'Eight Month army,' reflecting that their enlistments were scheduled to end on 31 December 1775. These regiments were composed on a small headquarters group, three field officer companies of 53 men and seven line companies of 60 men, totalling approximately 585. In addition, Massachusetts organised an artillery regiment of 10 companies.

New Hampshire

New Hampshire's contribution included three regiments, composed of 10 companies of 62 men in each. Rhode Island's 'Army of Observation' included three regiments, two organised with 10 companies of 60 men each and the third of nine companies and a company of artillery.

Rhode Island

Three regiments were authorised in May 1775 formed from existing county militia companies.

Connecticut

Connecticut created eight regiments of militia, six organised around ten 90-man companies and two with 65-man companies. The Connecticut Assembly initially authorised the creation of six regiments organised in a manner similar to Massachusetts followed by the organisation of two additional regiments of somewhat smaller size. Three of the regiments were sent to the Northern Department while the remaining five were assigned to Washington's army at Boston.

Delaware

Late in 1775 a single Continental regiment was organised.

New York

During the autumn of 1775, the focus of the war shifted from Boston to the Canadian frontier where New York formed four regiments of militia infantry and a company of artillery. The infantry companies included 76 soldiers. In September Colonel Benedict Arnold organised and led an expedition, composed of volunteers from the Cambridge army, through the Maine wilderness to support the offensive to capture Quebec. Arnold's force was composed of two volunteer battalions composed of five companies of 77 men each and three companies of riflemen, including Morgan's Virginia company.

Maryland

In August 1775 Maryland authorised the establishment of 40 companies of minutemen and reorganised the militia. In January 1776, the militia was disbanded and used to create a nine-company State Regiment composed of two artillery companies and seven infantry companies.

New Jersey

New Jersey raised two infantry regiments in June 1775 while Pennsylvania's House of Assembly approved the creation of 46 battalions of Associators. Maryland established 40 companies of minutemen in 1775 but amended this organisation in early 1776, by abolishing the minutemen and creating nine-company state regiments, made up of seven companies of infantry and two companies of artillery.

Pennsylvania

Rather than raise militia, the Pennsylvania House of Assembly instituted the Articles of Association of Pennsylvania in August 1775. As a result, 46 battalions of Associators were formed. In addition, the Council of Safety formed a company of artillery and in early March 1776 the Pennsylvania State Regiment of Riflemen and the Pennsylvania State Battalion of Musketry were created. In October 1776, these two regiments were consolidated into the Pennsylvania State Regiment.

In the southern colonies the formation and role of militia varied from the experience of the New England colonies. From Virginia to Georgia, the southern colonies had significant frontier boundaries to defend from periodic conflicts with Native American tribes. As settlers continued to migrate west across the Appalachian Mountains, frontier settlements were largely responsible for their own defences.

Virginia

In Virginia, Lord Dunmore's War of 1774 between the Shawnee Indian tribe and frontier settlers resulted in the raising of militia companies of varying size and organisation. After the Battle of Point Pleasant in October 1774, the Shawnee sued for peace. Many of the colonists that fought in both Dunmore's War and Regulators' War gained valuable practical military experience.

In response to the April 1775 British seizure of the public store of gunpowder from the magazine at Williamsburg, the Convention of Delegates organised two state regiments composed of militia companies along with three independent companies. The first regiment was composed of six companies armed with muskets and two companies

American militia defending a stone wall.

with rifles. The second regiment had five musket companies and two rifle companies. Each company was composed of 68 privates and nine officers and musicians. The independent companies were made up of 100 privates and 14 officers and musicians. The Convention raised the number of regiments to nine in December.

North Carolina

In addition, a series of internal conflicts in North Carolina between coastal landowners, supported by the British Royal Governor and settlers in the central and western regions, the Regulators, resulted in the Regulators War of 1768 and 1771. During these conflicts militia units were raised on both sides. In 1770 the colonial Governor called out militia companies from North Carolina's 29 counties. Each company was to have 59 men and were supplemented by independent companies of light infantry, rangers and light cavalry. The Regulators' companies turned out in force, but their formations were less organised and varied in size depending on local populations.

North Carolina organised the state into six military districts and agreed to raise two state regiments and six regiments of militia. All regiments were composed of 10 companies, each with 50 privates and three officers.

South Carolina

The South Carolina militia was organised into 12 regiments of infantry and one of cavalry. In 1775 South Carolina organised two infantry regiments and a mounted ranger regiment. The infantry regiments were organised along the British model, with eight centre companies, one light infantry company and one grenadier company. The regiments had 10 companies with 69 privates and 13 officers and musicians. The ranger regiment was to serve as mounted infantry and was composed of nine companies each with 50 privates and six officers and musicians.

In 1775 only a volunteer company of light infantry and one of grenadiers was organised at Savannah, although frontier militia companies existing on an ad hoc basis.

American militia dressed in a mix of coats and hunting shirts. 40mm Triguard figures.

Birth of the Continental Army 1775–1776

With the close of 1775 militia enlistments began to expire, beginning with Connecticut troops on 10 December, followed by the remainder of the militia outside Cambridge on 31 December.

Although beginning in 1776, the focus turned to the organisation of the Continental Army through the creation of regular infantry and cavalry regiments, militia units continued to play a major role in the war. Militia formations were used as pools to create the regiments required of each state by the Continental Congress. During each campaign American commanders relied on the response of local militias to supplement the meagre number of Continental units, particularly as the war wore on.

The American militia played a central role in harassing British and Loyalist foraging expeditions in New Jersey and Pennsylvania and challenging British control over the South Carolina back country after Continental formations were driven from the state. The overall quality of the militia increased over time as seasoned veterans of Continental units were mustered out of service at the end of their enlistments but returned to serve in militia formations, creating a core of veterans upon which the untrained militia could rely.

Continental Regiments

In addition to appointing George Washington as commander-in-chief in June 1775, the Continental Congress also established a number of positions intended to support the army at Cambridge. Adjutant General, Paymaster General, Commissary of Musters, Commissary General and Quartermaster General positions were created. Washington was assigned a military secretary, aides and engineers. A similar, although smaller command structure was approved for the New York army deployed around Fort Ticonderoga.

At the same time Congress created the ranks of major general and brigadier general, allowing each colony to nominate four major generals and eight brigadier generals. As the war progressed Washington sought Congressional approval to create the rank of lieutenant general, but without success.

Through the latter half of 1775, Washington and a Congressional Special Committee worked out plans to formalise an American army. Washington advised the committee that relying upon the uncertain motivation of militia formations was unsustainable. Anticipating resolution of the struggle with England would not last more than another year, the Committee proposed that enlistments and re-enlistments should be required for one year, terminating on 31 December 1776.

As part of this effort to organise the new Continental Army, Congress approved two different organisational structures for the new regiments. The October 1775 establishment to be used for regiments raised from New Jersey, Pennsylvania and Delaware included eight companies of 14 officers and musicians and 66 privates and a headquarters company of 13. Pennsylvania's regiments included seven companies armed with muskets and one with rifles.

The November 1775 organisation was to be used for regiments from other colonies and included eight companies with 14 officers and musicians but expanded the number of privates to 76, totalling 728 men. Maryland's regiment included a ninth company, of light infantry. In May Congress authorised the creation of the German Battalion, recruited from the German population in Maryland and Pennsylvania. The Battalion originally began with eight companies but subsequently added a ninth. In addition, Congress also authorised another rifle regiment composed of companies from Maryland and Virginia.

Table 1							
	October Establishment	November Establishment	1st Canadian Regiment - 2nd Canadian Regiment	Virginia Regiments	North Carolina Regiments	1st and 2nd SC - 5th and 6th SC	Georgia Regiments
1776 Establishment							
Headquarters Co.							
Colonel	1	1	1-1	1	1	1-1	1
Lt. Colonel	1	1	1-1	1	1	1-1	1
Major	1	1	1-1	1	1	1-1	1
Quartermaster	1	1	1-1	1	1	1-1	
Adjustant	1	1	1-1	1	1	1-1	1
Chaplain	1	1	1-1	1	1	1-	1
Surgeon	1	1	1-1	1	1	0-1	1
Surgeon's Mate	1	1	1-1	2	1	2-0	1
Sergeant Major	1	1	1-0	1	1	1-1	1
Quartermaster Sgt	1	1	1-0	1	1	0-1	1
Fife and Drum Sgt	1	1	1-0	1	1		2
Wagonmaster					1		
Commmissary of Stores					1		
Paymaster					1	0-1	1
Armorer						1-0	
Asistance Armorer						1-0	
Line Companies	8	8	8-5	10	8	10-3	8
Captain	1	1	1-0	1	1	1-0	1
1st Lieutenant	1	1	1-0	1	1	1-0	1
2nd Lieutenant	1	1			1	1-0	1
Ensign	1	1		1	1		1
Sergeant	1	4		4	4	3-0	4
Corporal	4	4	3-0	4	4	3-0	4
Fifer	1	1	1-0	1	1	2-0	1
Drummer	1	1	1-0	1	1	2-0	2
Privates	66	76	42	64	76	69	48

Detailed breakdown of the composition of various American regiments in 1776.

The reorganisation of the American Army took effect on 1 January 1776. The regiments raised in New England were given a numerical designation based on their colonel's relative seniority. The rifle companies from Pennsylvania, Maryland and Virginia were combined to form the 1st Continental Regiment.

Table 2 includes a list of the 27 Continental regiments, showing their 1775 origin and later dispositions in 1777.

Table 2	Continental Infantry Regiments 1776		
	1775 Status	1776 Designation	1777 Disposition
	1st Pennsylvania	1st Continental	1st Pennsylvania
	3rd New Hampshire	2nd Continental	3rd New Hampshire
	4th Massachusetts	3rd Continental	4th Massachusetts
	6th Massachusetts	4th Continental	6th Massachusetts
	1st New Hampshire	5th Continental	1st New Hampshire
	None	6th Continental	13th Massachusetts
	9th Massachusetts	7th Continental	Disbanded
	2nd New Hampshire	8th Continental	2nd New Hampshire
	1st Rhode Island	9th Continental	1st Rhode Island
	6th Connecticut	10th Continental	6th Connecticut
	2nd Rhode Island	11th Continental	2nd Rhode Island
	24th Massachusetts	12th Continental	Disbanded
	Read's MA Militia	13th Continental	None
	23rd Massachusetts	14th Continental	Disbanded
	Paterson's Militia	15th Continental	1st Massachusetts
	Sargent's Militia	16th Continental	8th Massachusetts
	Huntington's CT Militia	17th Continental	None
	Phinney MA Militia	18th Continental	12th Masschusetts
	Webb's CT Militia	19th Continental	None
	Durkee's CT Militia	20th Continental	None
	Ward's MA Militia	21st Continental	None
	Wyllys' CT Militia	22nd Continental	None
	Bailey' MA Militia	23rd Continental	2nd Massachusetts
	Greaton's MA Militia	24th Continental	3rd Massachusetts
	Bond's MA Militia	25th Continental	None
	Gerrish MA Militia	26th Continental	9th Massachusetts
	Hutchinson's MA	27th Continental	5th Massachusetts

Northern Department

In January 1776 Congress authorised the creation of an additional nine regiments for use in the Canadian Department, reorganised later in the year as the Northern Department. The 1st Canadians was to be composed of Canadians, while two would be

1st Canadian Regiment. The unit wore brown coats faced white and a leather cap with the inscription 'COR' Congress's Own Regiment. 40mm Triguard figures.

made up from veterans from the 1775 campaign. Six regiments were to be organised from New York, New Hampshire and Connecticut. All regiments were to be organised in the same structure as the other Continental regiments.

The 1st Canadian Regiment followed the November unit structure while the 2nd Canadian Regiment had a unique structure of two battalions, each of five companies, with one company possibly organised as light infantry. Throughout 1776 the situation in the Northern Department was fluid as Congress attempted to respond to the British invasion from Quebec. Additional regiments were authorised in New York and Continental regiments were sent north by Washington as events unfolded.

Middle Department

The Middle Department was created in February 1776 as a military administrative district embracing New York, New Jersey, Pennsylvania, Delaware and Maryland. While the bulk of Continental regiments were from New England, Pennsylvania, New Jersey, Maryland and Delaware also formed state regiments to supplement the Continental units.

Southern Department

Congress also requested the colonies of the Southern Department, Virginia, North and South Carolina and Georgia, to raise additional regiments, which were to retain their state designations.

Virginia

Virginia, asked to organise six regiments, was already in the process of forming nine regiments. Eight of the regiments were initially organised with seven companies, which was subsequently increased to 10. The ninth regiment began with seven companies but was also expanded to 10. The first seven regiments included seven musket companies and three rifle companies while the 8th and 9th regiments included only musket companies. Each company included 78 men: 64 privates and 14 officers and musicians. The regimental headquarters added 12 men. In addition, Virginia also maintained four independent companies of varying size at the western frontier forts.

Virginia also raised two companies of artillery, each with 65 men.

North Carolina

North Carolina organised six regiments, each with eight companies of 76 privates and 15 officers and musicians. Five independent companies were formed, two with full strength companies and with 60 privates rather than 76.

North Carolina's artillery company had 50 men.

South Carolina

South Carolina rejected the proposed Continental regimental organisation and maintained the previous organisation of the 1st and 2nd regiments, which included a light infantry and grenadier company. The 3rd (Ranger) regiment likewise maintained its organisation, adding an additional company. A 4th regiment composed primarily of artillery and intended for coastal defence had three companies, each with 111 men. The 5th South Carolina regiment had seven companies while the 6th had five. All companies had 92 privates and 11 officers.

28mm South Carolina State Regiment with distinctive leather cap.

Georgia

Georgia initially was asked by Congress to raise one regiment structured along the Continental model with eight companies, one being rifle armed. Congress also allowed Georgia to recruit three other regiments in Virginia, North Carolina and Pennsylvania. Each company included 48 privates and 15 officers and musicians, supported by a headquarters company of 13. A ranger regiment of 12 companies was organised following the South Carolina model. Two artillery batteries of 50 men were formed to protect Sunbury and Savannah.

Continental Artillery

In November 1775, Henry Knox was assigned command of the Continental artillery. On 2 December Congress stipulated that the Continental artillery regiment should be composed of 12 companies, commanded by a colonel, assisted by two lieutenant colonels and two majors. Each company was composed of five officers and 58 enlisted men and included eight guns divided into four sections.

Connecticut artillery and officer with 6pdr gun. 28mm Old Glory and Dixon figures.

The Flying Camp

To supplement the Continental regiments, Congress requested the formation of militia units from Pennsylvania, Maryland and Delaware into a 'flying camp' that would serve until 1 December 1776. In response, Pennsylvania created two units of state troops. The Pennsylvania State Musketry Battalion and a two battalion Pennsylvania State Rifle Regiment. In addition to the Pennsylvania contribution, additional militia units were organised including:

Haslet's 1st Battalion Flying Camp (Delaware)

Smallwood's 1st Regiment Flying Camp (Maryland)

Ewing's Maryland Flying Camp Regiment

Griffith's Maryland Flying Camp Regiment

Richardson's Flying Camp Regiment

American riflemen dressed in hunting shirts. 40mm Sash and Sabre and Triguard figures.

The Flying Camp was initially deployed around Wilmington, Delaware.

In August, Washington reorganised the main army into three 'grand divisions' including four brigades of Continental units and eight brigades of militia. By September, the main army had grown to 14 brigades. The September 1776 American Order of Battle, Table 4, provides a good example of the transition of the American army from the ragtag groups of militia that besieged Boston in 1775 and early 1776, to the reformed system of Continental regiments, supplemented by state and militia units.

In September 1776, the Americans had been defeated in the Battle of Brooklyn and forced to retreat to New York. After a short lull, British General Howe attempted to trap the Americans in New York by landing a British army at Kips Bay. The American army, escaped, retiring north to Harlem Heights. In addition to the American army at Harlem Heights American units occupied Fort Lee and Major General Gates had assembled a variety of units at Fort Ticonderoga to support the invasion of Canada.

Table 3 American Forces, September 1776		
Location: Harlem Heights, New York	**Unit**	**Strength**
Brigade: Parsons		
	7th Continentals (Mass)	234
	10th Continental (Conn)	314
	17th Continental (Conn)	137
	21st Continental (Mass)	190
	22nd Continental (Conn)	244
Brigade: George Clinton	Thomas NY Militia	301
	Graham NY Militia	200
	Swartout NY Militia	311
	Nicoll NY Militia	254
Brigade: Scott	Pawling NY Militia	347
	Lasher NY Militia	228
	Malcomb NY Militia	200
	Drake NY Militia	228
	Humphrey NY Militia	179
Brigade: Sargent	16th Continental (Mass)	325
	Ward's Connecticut	360
Brigade: Hand	1st Continental (PA)	300
	Haller Pennsylvania Flying Camp	431
	Cunningham Pennsylvania Flying Camp	184
Brigade: Wadsworth	2nd Connecticut State	264
	3rd Connecticut State	255
	4th Connecticut State	332
	1st Connecticut State	262
	5th Connecticut State	585
	Bradley's Connecticut State	256
Brigade: McDougall	19th Continental (Conn)	236
	1st New York	220
	3rd New York	314
	Smallwood's Maryland	510
Brigade: Heard	Van Cortland New Jersey Militia	225
	Martin New Jersey Militia	291
	Newcomb New Jersey Militia	315
	Forman New Jersey State	232
	Phillips New Jersey Militia	213
Brigade: Fellows	Holman Massachusetts Militia	375
	Cary Massachusetts Militia	367
	Smith Massachusetts Militia	419
Brigade: Beall	2nd Maryland Flying Camp	470
	3rd Maryland Flying Camp	394
	1st Maryland Flying Camp	558
	4th Maryland Flying Camp	449
Brigade: Mifflin	27th Continental (Mass)	313
	3rd Pennsylvania Battalion	410
	5th Pennsylvania Battalion	366
	Haslet Delaware	513
	Miles Rifle Regiment	171
	Atlee's Musketry Battalion	250

Unassigned	1st Virginia	406
	3rd Virginia	497
	6th Connecticut State	370
Location: Fort Lee, New Jersey		
Brigade: Nixon	4th Continental (Mass)	320
	9th Continental (RI)	244
	11th Continental (RI)	215
	12th Continental (Mass)	317
	23rd Continental (Mass)	268
Brigade: Glover	3rd Continental (Mass)	280
	13th Continental (Mass)	292
	14th Continental (Mass)	243
	26th Continental (Mass)	318
Northern Department		
Major General Horatio Gates		
Location: Fort Ticonderoga		
	24th Continental (Mass)	139
	25th Continental (Mass)	82
	Burrall Connecticut Regiment	120
	Porter Massachusetts Militia	88
	2nd Continental (NH)	153
	15th Continental (Mass)	211
	New Hampshire Rangers	174
	Wyman's New Hampshire	238
	5th Continental (NH)	220
	8th Continental (NH)	188
	2nd New Jersey	250
	Wingate's New Hampshire	232
	2nd Pennsylvania Battalion	294
	1st Pennsylvania Battalion	285
	Pennsylvania Independent Rifle Company	58
	1st New Jersey	296
	4th Pennsylvania Battalion	423
	6th Continental (Mass)	241
	Reed's Massachusetts Militia	302
	Wheelock's Massachusetts Militia	203
	Wigglesworth Massachusetts Militia	218
	Woodbridge's Massachusetts Militia	341
	Brewer's Massachusetts Militia	490
	Willard's Massachusetts Militia	341
	Swift Connecticut State Regiment	169
	6th Pennsylvania	249
	5th New York	199
	4th New York	31
	Mott's Connecticut State Regiment	236

In 1776 the newly organised Continental regiments formed only a portion of the American army. The army was still composed of a mix of militia and State regiments in addition to the Continental regiments.

40mm Sash and Sabre 1st Philadelphia Associators. Three battalions of Associators participated in the early 1777 campaign and fought at the Battle of Princeton.

American Continental artillery. 40mm Triguard and Sash and Sabre figures.

1777

Despite the decisions in 1776 to reorganise the American army, the results of the 1776 campaign highlighted the shortcomings of the army structure. In response, Congress and Washington made further modifications. Having found that the one-year enlistment period undermined the stability and reliability of the army, the recruitment period was extended to three years with cash bonuses and post-war land grants to be used as incentives.

In October 1776, a revised army organisation was approved, proposing the formation of 88 regiments drawn from each state based on relative populations. An additional six regiments were also identified, including the 1st and 2nd Canadian and the German regiment along with select formations from New York, Maryland and Pennsylvania. In December, this structure was further revised to add 16 'additional' regiments and three artillery regiments. All units were to be organised using the regimental and company structures authorised in the 1776 plan.

While the artillery regiments were administratively associated with a specific state, in most cases they were composed of individual artillery companies from different states.

Major John Lamb recruited in an area between Philadelphia and Connecticut and formed nine new companies, three from New York, two from Pennsylvania and four from Connecticut. These were added to three existing companies, including Alexander Hamilton's New York company and the remnants of Lamb's former company. The composition of each artillery company was modified, reducing the number of guns from eight to six along with associated personnel. During the 1776 campaign two- and four-gun artillery sections, usually 3pdr and 4pdr guns, were assigned to each brigade, a policy that continued throughout the war. Larger calibre cannon, 6pdr and 12pdr field guns, were concentrated in a central artillery park.

Also included in the new army structure was the creation of four regiments of light dragoons. Each regiment would have a headquarters troop of 13 and six troops of 44 men.

American 1st Light Dragoons in 1781 uniform. 40mm Sash and Sabre.

Table 4 1777 American Army

State	Infantry	Artillery	Light Dragoon Cavalry
New Hampshire	3 Regiments		
Massachusetts	15 Regiments	1 Regiment	
Rhode Island	2 Regiments		
Connecticut	8 Regiments	½ Regiment	1 Regiment
New York	4 Regiments	½ Regiment	
New Jersey	4 Regiments		
Pennsylvania	12 Regiment	1 Regiment	1 Regiment
Delaware	1 Regiment		
Maryland	8 Regiments		
Virginia	15 Regiments	1 Regiment	2 Regiments
North Carolina	9 Regiments		
South Carolina	6 Regiments		
Georgia	1 Regiment		

1777 American Supplemental Units

Formation	Composition
Warner's Continental Regiment	Recruited from New York and New Hampshire
German Battalion	Pennsylvania and Maryland
1st and 2nd Canadian Regiments	1st Regiment included 8 companies while the 2nd Regiment was composed of two battalions, each of five companies.
Dubois Regiment	Recruited in New York's Hudson Highlands
Maryland/Virginia Rifle Regiment	Recruited in Maryland and Virginia

1777 "Additional" Regiments

Formation	Recruitment Areas
Gist's Ranger Corps	Virginia/ Maryland-four companies
Foreman's Additional	New Jersey/Maryland
Grayson's Additional	Maryland/Virginia
Hartley's Additional	Pennsylvania/Maryland
Henley's Additional	Massachusetts
Jackson's Additional	Massachusetts
Lee's Additional	Massachusetts
Malcom's Additional	New York
Patton's Additional	Pennsylvania/Maryland
Rawling's Additional	Virginia
Sherburne's Additional	Maryland/Connecticut
Thurston's Additional	Virginia
Webb's Additional	Connecticut

The 1777 reorganisation of the American army assigned quotas to individual states and established supplemental and 'Additional' regiments.

Washington took the opportunity to formalise the army's command structure, specifying one brigadier general for every three regiments and one major general for every three brigades.

While states in the Southern Department were required to raise regiments to serve in Washington's main army operating in New Jersey and Pennsylvania, additional combat units were also organised. Virginia raised three regiments and an artillery regiment assigned to coastal defence within the state.

1778

As the war continued, Congress sought to reduce costs and allow regiments to reflect a more realistic effective strength. The 16 'Additional' regiments were permitted to be assigned to state quotas. The 1778 Continental regiments were reorganised and as a result of the reduction in officers from 40 to 29, the composition of individual companies could vary.

Since British colonels rarely took the field with their regiments, making the exchange of captured officers on an equivalent basis problematic, the American restructuring included the elimination of the position of colonel within each regiment. Existing colonels were able to retain their positions, but vacancies were not filled. While each company fielded 65 men, two or three companies operated with a different command structure. The number of privates in each company was reduced to 53 from the previous establishment of either 66 or 76 privates.

In addition, each regiment was expanded to nine companies by adding a light infantry company organised as the other companies. The reorganisation reduced the paper strength of regiments by 30 percent. The 2nd Canadian Regiment maintained its unique structure of two battalions each of five companies, while the 1st Canadian Regiment adopted a similar organisation although of only one battalion.

Webb's Additional Continental Regiment initially wore captured British uniforms, red coats with yellow facings. 28mm Old Glory.

The reorganisation also expanded the strength of the light dragoon regiments, increasing each cavalry troop to four officers and 64 men. Formal engineering companies of 71 men were also established. Table 5 provides details of the organisation of the Continental infantry regiments cavalry regiments and organisation of units of the Southern Department.

Table 5			
	Continental Infantry Regiment	1777 Light Dragoon	1778 Light Dragoon
1778			
Headquarters Co.			
Colonel	1	1	1
Lt. Colonel	1	1	1
Major	1	1	1
Quartermaster	1	1	1
Adjutant	1	1	1
Paymaster	1	1	1
Surgeon	1	1	1
Surgeon's Mate	1	1	1
Sergeant Major	1		
Quartermaster Sgt	1		
Fife and Drum Sgt	2		
Trumpet Major		1	1
Chaplain		1	
Riding Master		1	1
Saddler		1	1
Cadets in Training		4	
Line Companies	9	6	6
Captain	1	1	1
1st Lieutenant	1	1	2
Ensign	1		
Cornet		1	1
Sergeant	3	1	2
Quartermaster Sgt		1	1
Corporal	3	4	5
Fifer	1		
Trumpeter		1	2
Farrier		1	2
Drummer	1		
Armorer		1	
Privates	53	32	54

The 1778 American army reorganisation modified the composition of infantry and light dragoon regiments

The issue of recruitment and ongoing manpower shortages came to a head because of the 1777 Continental army reorganisation. Each state was given a quota and enlistments were expanded to three years or the duration of the war. The exception to this were six North Carolina and nine Virginia Regiments, all formed in 1776 with enlistments expiring in 1778 or early 1779. To respond to the shortfalls in recruitment, state militias divided their men into classes of from 15 to 20 men, then called out, or drafted, one or several of a county's classes for service ranging from weeks to months. Continental regiments were often augmented from state militia drafts. In January 1778, Washington reported to a Congressional Conference Committee that voluntary enlistments would not be able to fill the vacancies in the regiments and that drafts from the militia, while disagreeable, would be necessary. In February, the Continental Congress resolved to require all states, except for South Carolina and Georgia, to fill up their Continental regiments with militia drafts. This programme was undertaken in the spring and summer with mixed results.

1779

Beginning in late 1778 and continuing through 1779, the individual states implemented the revised structure of the Continental Army. In early 1779 Congress adjusted the total number of regiments to 80, reducing the quotas from several states. To meet their quotas some states consolidated existing regiments and integrated elements of the 'Additional' regiments to fill out the Continental regiments.

American Continental regiment dressed in blue coats with yellow facings. 40mm Sash and Sabre.

1780

In early 1780, Congress, acting on recommendations from Washington and consistent with the minimum rank and file strength of 324 for each regiment stipulated by Stueben, established a total Continental quota of 35,211, which included infantry, cavalry and artillery. The transfer of veteran regiments to the Southern Department, coupled with shortfalls in recruitment and the unavailability of recently arrived French forces, forced Washington to cancel plans to attack New York City. In October, shaken by the surrender of Charleston and defeat at Camden, Congress approved a reorganisation of the American army.

The April 1780 American Order of Battle, Table 6, reflects the full implementation of the 1777 Continental army reorganisation and the distribution of forces between the Northern Department and Southern Department. Troop strengths vary, with the militia units no bigger than several companies, but most Continental regiments were still well under their full establishment strength. In May 1780, the Charleston garrison surrendered to British forces after a brief siege.

Table 6 American Forces, April, 1780		
Location: Morristown, New Jersey	**Unit**	**Strength**
Brigade: Irvine	1st Pennsylvania	186
	2nd Pennsylvania	295
	7th Pennsylvania	137
	10th Pennsylvania	218
Brigade: 2nd Pennsylvania	3rd Pennsylvania	209
	5th Pennsylvania	219
	6th Pennsylvania	161
	9th Pennsylvania	119
Brigade: Hand	4th Pennsylvania	168
	11th Pennsylvania	241
	2nd Canadian	292
	1st Canadian	91
Brigade: Maxwell	1st New Jersey	143
	2nd New Jersey	178
	3rd New Jersey	
	Spencer's Additional	82
Brigade: Clinton	2nd New York	127
	5th New York	150
	4th New York	151
	3rd New York	271
Brigade: Parsons	3rd Connecticut	231
	4th Connecticut	105
	6th Connecticut	318
	8th Connecticut State	156
Brigade: Huntington	1st Connecticut	124
	2nd Connecticut	89
	5th Connecticut	131
	7th Connecticut	143
Brigade: Stark	2nd Rhode Island	232
	Sherburne's Additional	104
	Webb's Additional	150
	Jackson's Additional	272
Artillery	2nd Continental (eight companies)	200
	3rd Continental (seven companies)	116
	4th Continental (eight companies)	119
Location: Highlands, N.Y.		
Brigade: Nixon	3rd Massachusetts	80
	5th Massachusetts	121
	6th Massachusetts	114
	12th Massachusetts	135

Brigade: Glover	1st Massachusetts	137
	4th Massachusetts	158
	13th Massachusetts	119
	15th Massachusetts	73
Brigade: Patterson	7th Massachusetts	96
	10th Massachusetts	103
	11th Massachusetts	79
	14th Massachusetts	77
Brigade: 4th Massachusetts	2nd Massachusetts	158
	8th Massachusetts	80
	9th Massachusetts	113
Brigade: Poor	1st New Hampshire	181
	2nd New Hampshire	161
	3rd New Hampshire	129
Unassigned	1st New York	257
	Warner's Additional	77
Southern Department: Major General Lincoln		
Location: Charleston, S.C.		
Brigade: Hogun	1st North Carolina	194
	2nd North Carolina	243
	3rd North Carolina	86
Brigade: Woodford	1st Virginia	307
	3rd Virginia	246
	2nd Virginia	309
Brigade: Scott	1st Virginia Detachment	157
	2nd Virginia Detachment	214
	2nd South Carolina	79
	3rd South Carolina	151
	Lytle's North Carolina Militia	175
Brigade: McIntosh	Maybank S.C. Militia	14
	Garden S.C. Militia	65
	Skirving S.C. Militia	28
	McDonald's S.C. Militia	87
	Giles S.C. Militia	72
	Hicks S.C. Militia	16
	Richardson's S.C. Militia	57
	Kershaw's S.C. Militia	26
	Goodwin's S.C. Militia	37
	Harrington's N.C. Militia	135
	Tinning's N.C. Militia	84
Brigade: Simons	1st Btn. Charleston Militia	222
	2nd Btn. Charleston Militia	210
	Bretigny's Corps	85
Artillery	4th South Carolina	105
	Independent Continental Company	32
	Charleston Btn.	137

Although not as diverse as the composition of the American army in 1776, the 1780 army was organised around state regiments and militia and still composed a significant portion of American forces, particularly in the Southern Department.

1781

The adopted Congressional Plan required that, as of 1 January 1781, the regular army was to consist of 49 infantry regiments, the special Canadian regiment, four legionary corps, two partisan corps and a regiment of artificers. The Congressional plan assigned each regiment, except the Canadian regiment and the partisan corps, to a specific state. Table 7 provides a summary of the quotas for each state.

Table 7 1781 Continental State Quotas				
State	**Infantry Regiments**	**Artillery Regiments**	**Legionary Corps**	**Partisan Corps**
New Hampshire	2			
Massachusetts	10	1		
Rhode Island	1			
Connecticut	5		1	
New York	2	1		
New Jersey	2			
Pennsylvania	6	1	1	
Maryland	5			
Delaware	1			
Virginia	8	1	2	
North Carolina	4			
South Carolina	2			
Georgia	1			
Unallocated	1			2

While the 1781 quotas for individual states was reduced from previous years it now included artillery and legionary formations.

After modifying the structure of each regiment, including additional officers, non-commissioned officers (NCOs) and privates, each regiment, still composed of eight line companies and a light infantry company, totalling 709, with 544 rank and file.

American artillery was organised into four regiments, each of 10 companies and the number of matrosses was increased in each company. Congress adopted Washington's proposal to revise the organisation of the light dragoon regiments by designating two of the six companies as dismounted. Washington also proposed the creation of partisan regiments, composed of three mounted troops and three dismounted troops. One of the partisan corps was allocated to Washington's main army and the other sent to the Southern Department. Table 6 summarises the 1781 reorganisation of infantry, cavalry, artillery and legions.

American Continental regiment uniforms, a mix of brown coats with red facings and hunting shirts. 40mm Sash and Sabre.

Table 8				
	Continental Infantry Regiment	**Artillery Regiment**	**Legionary Corps**	**Partisan Corps**
1781 Reorganisation				
Headquarters Co.				
Colonel	1	1	1	1
Lt. Colonel	1	1	1	1
Major	1	1	1	1
Quartermaster	1	1	1	1
Adjutant	1	1	1	1
Paymaster	1	1	1	1
Surgeon	1	1	1	1
Surgeon's Mate	1	1	1	1
Sergeant Major	1	1		
Quartermaster Sgt	1	1		
Fife and Drum Sgt	2			
Drum Major	1	1		
Fife Major	1	1		
Recruiter	1			
Saddler			1	1
Riding Master			1	1
Trumpet Major			1	1
Companies	9	10	6	6
Captain	1	1	1	1
Captain Lieutenant		1		
1st Lieutenant	1	1	1	1
2nd Lieutenants		3	1	1
Ensign	1			
Cornet			1	1
1st Sergeant	1			
Sergeant	4	6	2	2
Quartermaster Sgt			1	1
Corporal	4	6	5	5
Fifer	1	1		
Trumpeter			1	1
Farrier			1	1
Drummer	1	1		
Armorer				
Bombardiers		6		
Gunners		6		
Matrosses		39		
Privates	64		60	50

In 1781 the organisation of infantry, light dragoon, artillery and legions was again modified.

Implementation of these reorganisations began in January 1781. Disputes about chronic shortages of food, clothing and pay, coupled with confusion over the consolidation of existing regiments and ongoing misunderstandings about enlistments, led to the mutiny of several regiments, beginning with troops from Pennsylvania followed by those from New Jersey. Congress mollified the Pennsylvania mutineers by releasing or furloughing approximately 2,400 men. The New Jersey revolt was put down with harsher methods and several ringleaders were executed.

American Continental artillery section with limber. 28mm Old Glory.

Post Yorktown

With the surrender of Cornwallis' army in October 1781, the war began to wind down and while skirmishes continued, particularly in the Southern Department, the Continental army was slowly dismantled throughout 1782. Continuing tension between the American Army and Continental Congress in 1783 over back pay and a call for expanded furloughs resulted in further reductions in the army.

Legions

Partisan corps or legions were also established as part of the 1778 reorganisation. In late 1777, Baron von Ottendorf was authorised to raise one company of light infantry and two companies of riflemen. A fourth company was added in early 1777. Colonel Armand Tuffin later assumed command of the unit. Each company was intended to field four officers, eight non-commissioned officers, two musicians and 128 privates.

Pulaski's Legion infantry, dressed in a mix of official uniforms, blue coats with red facings and hunting shirts. 40mm Triguard.

Lee's Legion, organised by Major Henry Lee using the original light dragoon organisation, with three troops, each composed of 12 officers and support personnel and 32 privates. In 1779 Captain Allen McLane's light infantry company was added as a fourth company. Lee's Legion was redesignated a Partisan Legion in 1780 and reorganised to include three mounted and three dismounted troops.

Brigadier General Casimir Pulaski was authorised to raise a legion during the summer of 1778. Pulaski's Legion included one troop of lancers, two troops of light dragoons, one company of riflemen and two companies of light infantry. There is evidence that a company of grenadiers were also part of the Legion.

Militia

As the conflict in the Northern Department wound down after the British evacuation of Philadelphia in 1778, the war moved south and in the Middle and Southern Departments, militia played a key role for the Americans. Significant militia formations supported the efforts of the Continental forces, particularly during the 1780 and 1781 campaigns.

In the Middle Department the New Jersey militia responded to the 1780 incursion from New York.

In the south, after the debacle of the surrender of 6,000 troops at Charleston, many militia leaders and their men were paroled and returned to their homes. The subsequent actions of the British to require declarations of loyalty violated the terms of the parole and allowed the formation of new militia units. Militia units from Virginia, North Carolina and South Carolina joined the nucleus of the reformed Continental army in August 1780.

The disastrous battle of Camden resulted in the retreat of organised Continental forces from South Carolina. South Carolina militia units continued to harass Loyalist outposts and British foraging parties while Major General Nathanael Greene reorganised the American army in North Carolina. Unlike militia units at the beginning of the war which were largely composed of untrained or partially trained volunteers with little military experience, the militia mustered later in the war included a core of former Continental veterans who had completed their formal service. These veterans helped train the other recruits and improved the reliability of the militia units.

At the battle of King's Mountain in October 1780 an army composed entirely of militia from North Carolina, Virginia and South Carolina defeated a British force composed entirely of Loyalist units.

In early 1781, militia from the Carolinas and Virginia supplemented a core of Continental troops to defeat Lieutenant Colonel Tarleton at Cowpens. Large numbers of militia from Virginia and North Carolina supplemented Greene's army throughout early 1781, culminating with the Battle of Guilford Courthouse in March. When Greene moved into South Carolina later in 1781, he was supported by South Carolina militia. Virginia militia formed a part of the American army that besieged Lieutenant General Cornwallis at Yorktown in September 1781.

American mounted militia infantry. Most militia in the Southern Department moved by horse, dismounting to fight on foot. 40mm Triguard.

American Tactical Doctrine

For the most part American officers at the start of the war had very little formal military training or practical experience. Aside from those militia officers or former Crown officers, who had fought in the French and Indian War and may have had some experience with Edward Harvey's *Manual Exercise as Ordered by his Majesty in 1764*, American officers had to rely on studying several military manuals that were available as the war began.

In the southern colonies, Colonel Bland's *A Treatise of Military Discipline,* originally published in 1727, was frequently updated. In 1775 General Washington recommended the use of the most recent edition of the *Treatise* when asked about training manuals.

The Virginia Convention directed the use of the 1764 British *Manual* for both state and militia regiments. Brigadier General McDougall requested training advice from Washington in May 1777. Although Washington supported McDougall's plan for training, highlighting the need for uniformity among regiments, he did not recommend a specific manual. Left to his own decision McDougall adopted the 1764 British *Manual.* In response to a similar question from Colonel Alexander Spotswood of the 2nd Virginia Regiment in April 1777, Washington made no specific recommendation but advised Spotswood to drill his men at every opportunity and focus on field manoeuvres rather than the manual of arms. Washington highlighted marching, wheeling in order and the platoon exercise as primary objectives, dismissing the other drills as more useful for the parade ground rather than actual combat.

American Continental regiment deployed in line. 40mm Sash and Sabre.

Nicolas Lewis, a merchant from Philadelphia who had served as a British officer, wrote *A Treatise of Military Exercise, Calculated for the Use of the Americans*, published in 1776 and dedicated to the commanders of Philadelphia militia. Lewis' work covered similar material as the British *Manual Exercise*, addressing manoeuvring and firing. It is interesting to note that Lewis argued strongly against adopting the two-rank formation, recommending the Philadelphia militia continue to use a three-rank line formation. In June 1777, Lewis was appointed commander of the American Invalid Corps, which he led until 1782.

The *Norfolk Discipline*, written by William Windham was circulating in New England military circles as early as 1764 when an abstract was published in Boston. Thomas Pickering published a simplified version, *Easy Plan of Discipline for Militia* which was widely used in the northern colonies early in the war. The *Norfolk Discipline*, published in 1759, was intended for the training of militia and addressed the manual of arms, facing and firing. The firing section included drills for rapid firing, firing by alternate platoons, firing on the advance and firing on the retreat. Also included were manoeuvres for platoons such as wheeling, oblique march, opening or closing of the ranks and a bayonet drill. An updated version was printed in 1775 and published in a variety of locations including New York, Philadelphia, Baltimore and Lancaster.

The Massachusetts Provincial Congress adopted the 1764 British Manual in 1774, which was also in general use among units in Connecticut, Rhode Island and Massachusetts Bay.

German Captain Ewald wrote in 1777 that he was impressed by the military reading material he found in captured American officers' knapsacks or trunks. He mentioned works by Frederick the Great, translated into English in London in 1762 and *A Treatise on the Military Service of Light Horse and Light Infantry* by Major General de Grandmaison and translated in 1777.

While Windham's *Norfolk Discipline* was the adopted training manual for North Carolina troops in 1775 and in 1776, the North Carolina Committee of Safety requested copies of *The Military Guide for Young Officers* by Thomas Simes, along with *A New System of Military Discipline, Founded Upon Principle* (by Richard Lambart, Earl of Cavan.)

Despite the general impression that American units were untrained until von Steuben's *Blue Book*, the widespread availability and use of various training manuals prior to 1778 suggests the regiments of the Continental army in 1776 and 1777 were able to conduct complicated battlefield manoeuvres. The use of different training manuals did result in a lack of uniformity in the manoeuvres between units of the same brigade and between brigades.

Baron von Steuben's Reforms

In early 1778 Washington assigned the newly arrived Baron Frederick von Steuben responsibility for preparing a system of 'discipline, manoeuvres, evolutions [and] regulations for Guards'. Von Steuben used the 1764 British manual as the basis to develop a new set of regulations to train the Continental troops. He simplified the British manual of arms, modified the structure of the column of march to allow for more compact formations, which facilitated battlefield deployments. He also increased the marching rate from the English 60 two-foot steps per minute to the Prussian standard of 75 and prescribed double time at 120 steps. Von Steuben directed that Continental units deploy into two-rank, closed formations and stipulated units march in closed columns, protected by their light infantry company, before deploying into line.

Using the existing eight company regimental structure, von Steuben subdivided each regiment of at least 320 men, into two four-company battalions, led by either the Colonel or Lieutenant Colonel, while smaller regiments were intended to be combined.

In preparation for the 1780 campaign, von Steuben provided recommendations to both Washington and Congressional Committees proposing regiments be composed of nine companies, eight regular companies and one light infantry company, each of 36 men. These regiments, totalling 324 each, should be organised into brigades of four regiments. He also proposed that the light cavalry regiments be composed of three squadrons of 68 men each. Each squadron should be organised into two companies of 34.

American Continental infantry brigade of four regiments deployed for battle. 28mm Old Glory.

Light Infantry

From the beginning of the war the American Army included units designated as light infantry, ranging from a single company to a regiment. These units were consolidated at various times on an ad hoc basis for specific campaigns but never as a formal organisation. While these units were referred to as light infantry, they were not trained in formal light infantry tactics, were composed primarily of rifle armed troops and usually operated as scouts or advance guards. The 1st Continental regiment of 1776 was composed of the various rifle companies commanded by Colonel Daniel Morgan.

In May 1777 Washington instructed Colonel Morgan to organise a battalion of riflemen from Maryland, Pennsylvania and Virginia regiments. Morgan's unit conformed to the eight company structure, totalling 578 men and officers. After dispatching Morgan's regiment to the Northern Department in August, Washington ordered each brigade in Stephen's, Greene's and Lincoln's divisions to form two companies totalling 117 men. The four companies from each division composed a battalion, led by a lieutenant colonel. Washington assigned command of the newly formed light infantry to Brigadier General William Maxwell throughout the 1777 campaign, and it was then disbanded when Morgan's corps returned to the main army.

In 1778, leading up to the battle of Monmouth, Washington utilised Morgan's rifle corps to maintain contact with the British army as it retired from Philadelphia. He also formed units of 'picked men' to lead the main Continental army advance.

The 1779 Continental regimental reorganisation added a light infantry company to each regiment. In preparation for the assault on Stony Point, the light infantry companies were withdrawn into composite battalions. As a result, four battalions of four companies each were formed under the command of Brigadier General Anthony Wayne. Wayne's appointment infuriated Colonel Morgan who coveted command of the light infantry, leading to his resignation from the army.

After the successful action at Stony Point, the light infantry companies were returned to their parent regiments, but in late 1780 Washington formally created a separate light infantry corps under the command of the Marquis de Lafayette. These light infantry battalions were considered elite shock troops, similar to British grenadier and light infantry companies.

American riflemen dressed in hunting shirts. The colour of hunting shirts varied widely and included greens, blues and purples. 40mm Sash and Sabre.

In January 1781, the light infantry corps was proposed to be organised by detaching a light infantry company composed of 25 rank and file and nine officers and musicians. In February, these orders were amended to increase the size of the company to five sergeants and 50 rank and file and three battalions each of eight companies were formed The first battalion was composed of eight companies from the Massachusetts regiments. The second battalion included two companies from Massachusetts regiments, five from Connecticut and one from Rhode Island. The third battalion included five New Jersey, two New Hampshire and one company from Hazen's Canadian Regiment. These battalions marched to Virginia under Lafayette's command and joined the main Continental army during the siege of Yorktown.

A second light infantry corps was organised during the summer, composed of two battalions, using the same company structure as Lafayette's battalions, one with eight companies, the other with six.

Artillery

The reorganisation of 1781 reduced the number of regiments to 29 regiments and Artillery.

Major General Knox reorganised the American artillery, assigning four 3pdr or 6pdr guns to each brigade and establishing an artillery park of guns of larger calibre. In addition, an unmanned artillery reserve of 24pdr, 12pdr, 6pdr and 3pdr guns was assigned to the main army train. A siege train was also organised. Knox stipulated extended training for artillery crews and promoted the doctrine of engaging enemy infantry rather than enemy artillery.

Light Dragoons

Von Stueben's 1778 manual was primarily focused on the training of infantry units rather than cavalry. Von Steuben's cavalry training manual was published in 1794, too late for use in the Revolution and even then, was considered incomplete. While British manuals may have been used, they typically addressed training for both heavy and light cavalry.

Count Casimir Pulaski, when appointed to command all American light dragoons in 1777, ordered the regiments to translate and adopt the Prussian cavalry training drill. In addition, Pulaski appointed Michael Kovats as riding master. Kovats was a former officer of Prussian hussars and a veteran of the Seven Years War. British officers also included William Fawcett's English translation of the *Regulations for the Prussian Cavalry*, published in 1757, available for reference.

In 1780 shortages of forage and horses forced Washington to disperse the Continental light dragoons. The 1st and 3rd Regiments were transferred to the Southern Department and operated as a composite unit for the remainder of the war. The 2nd and 4th Regiments redeployed a portion of their troopers as infantry.

British Army Organisation and Training

In 1774 there were 70 British regiments of foot; household regiments and regiments of the line, most with one battalion composed of a headquarter and 10 companies. The 1st (Royal Scots) and 60th (Royal Americans) had two battalions. Each battalion included eight musketeer or line companies, one grenadier and one light infantry company. The line and light companies totalled 47 men; 38 privates along with a drummer, five NCOs, led by a captain and two lieutenants. The grenadier company included two fifers rather than a drummer. While regiments tended to be close to full strength prior to being deployed, once overseas they seldom received drafts and over time would see their strength diminish.

The household regiments included the Foot Guards, composed of the 1st, 2nd and 3rd Regiments of Foot Guards. In addition, there were two regiments of Household Cavalry - the 1st and 2nd Lifeguards.

The War Begins

At the start of 1774 there were approximately 13 regiments along with five companies of the Royal Artillery stationed in British North America. The regiments, sometimes broken into separate companies, were scattered across Canada in the cities and along the frontiers of the 13 colonies and in Florida. At the request of General Sir Thomas Gage, four additional regiments were sent as reinforcements and two battalions of marines were organised by the Royal Navy. After the British retreat to Halifax after the evacuation of Boston, Howe left the marine battalions as part of the garrison, although their light and grenadier companies continued to serve with the main army.

Beginning in 1775, the need to expand the regular army resulted in the expansion of existing regiments and the creation of new regiments. As a result of this expansion in existing regiments, each company now included 67 men, 56 privates, two musicians and seven NCOs, led by a captain and lieutenant. Table 9 provides detail on British and German regimental organisation.

American Continental 2nd Light Dragoons wearing blue jackets with buff facings. 40mm Sash and Sabre.

Table 9				
	Hesse Cassel 1776	British 1775	British New Regiments 1778	British Foot Guards
Headquarters Co.				
Colonel	1	1	1	1
Lt. Colonel	1	1	1	1
Major	1	1	1	1
Quartermaster	1	1	1	1
Judge Advocate	1			
Chaplain	1	1	1	1
Surgeon	1	1	1	1
Surgeon's Mate		1	1	1
Armorer	1	1	1	1
Musicians	6	1	1	1
Assistant Provost	1	1	1	1
Adjutant		1	1	1
Wagonmaster	1			
Commmissary of Stores				
Paymaster				
Armorer	1			
Asistance Armorer				
Line Companies	5	8	8	8
Captain	1	1	1	1
Lieutenants	2	1	2	1
Quartermaster Sgt.	1			
Provost Sgt.	1			
Ensign	1	1		1
Sergeant	3	3	3	3
Clerk	1			
Corporal	7	3	3	4
Officer Servants	4			1
Drummer	3	2	2	1
Privates	105	53	100	93
Grenadier Company	1	1		1
Captain	1	1	1	1
Lieutenants	2	2	3	2
Quartermaster Sgt.	1			
Provost Sgt.	1			
Ensign	1			
Clerk	1			
Sergeant	3	3	5	3
Corporal	7	3	5	3
Fifer		2		2
Drummer	3	2		2
Piper			2	

Privates	105	53	100	120
Light Company		1	1	1
Captain	1	1		1
Lieutenants	1	2	3	2
Quartermaster Sgt				
Provost Sgt				
Ensign				
Clerk				
Sergeant	2	3	5	3
Corporal		3	5	3
Fifer				
Hornest		2		2
Piper			2	
Privates	105	53	100	96

British regiment of foot with yellow facings. 40mm Sash and Sabre and Triguard.

While each regiment had a compliment of drummers and fifers, or pipers in Highland regiments, it is unclear how much these musicians were engaged in transmitting orders on the battlefield.

Throughout the course of the war additional formations were organised for service in America. In 1775 four new battalions were raised, two of which were assigned to the 71st (Highland) Regiment of Foot, while the 60th Foot was expanded by two battalions.

As part of the reinforcements, Howe was sent a brigade of Guards. The Guards were organised as an oversized battalion complete with flank companies. The line companies included 93 privates, two musicians, nine NCOs, a lieutenant and captain. The light infantry company was organised slightly differently, with 96 privates, while the grenadier company was larger with 120 privates. (See Table 9). The battalion, which had been trained using the 1764 drill, was reorganised by Howe into two battalions and retrained using the revised light infantry tactical doctrine. In 1779 the Guards brigade added two flank companies; a light infantry company for the 1st battalion and a grenadier company for the 2nd battalion. The number of line companies for each battalion was reduced from four to three.

Table 10 British Forces, August 1776		
Location: Staton Island	**Units**	**Strength**
	17th Light Dragoons	300
Brigade: BG Leslie	1st Light Infantry (4th, 5th, 10th, 17th,22nd, 23rd, 27th, 35th, 38th)	415
	2nd Light Infantry (40th, 43rd, 44th, 45th, 46th, 49th, 52nd, 55th, 63rd, 64th)	416
	3rd Light Infantry (15th, 28th, 33rd, 37th, 46th, 54th 57th)	284
Brigade: BG Matthews	1st Guards Battalion	500
	2nd Guards Battalion	500
1st Brigade: MG Robinson	4th Foot	252
	15th Foot	300
	27th Foot	319
	45th Foot	314
2nd Brigade: MG Pigot	5th Foot	292
	28th Foot	300
	35th Foot	308
	52nd Foot	324
3rd Brigade: MG Jones	10th Foot	292
	37th Foot	307
	38th Foot	340
	52nd Foot	284
4th Brigade: MG Grant	17th Foot	307
	40th Foot	350
	46th Foot	283
	55th Foot	314

5th Brigade: BG Smith	22nd Foot	329
	43rd Foot	290
	54th Foot	327
	63rd Foot	292
6th Brigade: BG Agnew	23rd Foot	299
	44th Foot	279
	57th Foot	324
	64th Foot	321
Brigade: BG Erskine	1/71st Highland	500
	2/71st Highland	500
	3/71st Highland	500
Reserve: Lt General Cornwallis	1st Grenadier (4th, 5th, 10th, 17th, 22nd, 23rd, 27th, 35th, 38th, 40th)	438
	2nd Grenadier (43rd, 44th, 45th, 49th, 52nd, 55th, 63rd, 64th , 1st Marine, 2nd Marine)	392
	3rd Grenadier (15th, 28th, 33rd, 37th, 46th, 54th, 57th)	319
	4th Highland Grenadier (42nd, 71st)	284
	33rd Foot	315
	42nd Highland	606
Royal Artillery: BG Cleveland	1st Battalion (2 companies)	180
	2nd Battalion (2 companies)	180
	3rd Battalion (8 companies)	600
Hessian Division: Lt. General von Heister		
	Hesse Cassel Artillery	200
Brigade: MG Von Mirbach	Von Knyphausen Fusiliers	600
	Von Rall Grenadier Battalion	500
	Lieb Musketeers	600
	Von Lossburg Fusiliers	600
Brigade: MG Stirn	Von Donop Musketeers	600
	Von Mirbach Musketeers	600
	Erbprinz Fusiliers	600
Brigade: Colonel Von Donop	Von Block Grenadier Battalion	500
	Von Minnigerode Grenadier Battalion	500
	Von Linsingen Grenadier Battalion	500
	Hesse Cassel Jaegers	220
Brigade: Von Lossberg	Von Ditfurth Fusiliers	600
	Von Tuurmbach Musketeers	600
	Prinz Karl Musketeers	600

In August 1776, the British army was composed of foot regiments, composite light infantry and grenadier battalions and a large component of German troops.

Due to losses incurred during the 1776 campaign, the 6th and 14th Regiments of Foot were disbanded. Their remaining rank and file were redistributed to other regiments as replacements, while the officers and NCOs returned to England to recruit and rebuild the regiments. No new regiments were raised in 1776 but in 1777 five Highland battalions were organised. These included the 73rd Highlanders with two battalions, the 74th, 76th and 77th. With the entry of France into the war as an ally of the United States, the nature of the war expanded and required additional resources.

After evacuating Philadelphia and returning to New York in 1778, the 16th Light Dragoons together with the 10th, 45th and 52nd Foot returned to England, although their enlisted men were redistributed as replacements to remaining regiments in America. The two marine battalions defending Halifax were withdrawn to England and nine foot regiments, along with their light infantry and grenadier companies, were also embarked for service in the West Indies. The loss of these units forced Clinton in 1779 to reconstitute the light and grenadier battalions. Flank companies from the garrisons at Newport and Halifax were ordered to New York. In September 1779, the 76th and 80th Foot arrived as reinforcements. At the same time officers and senior NCOs of the 26th Foot returned to England and the enlisted men remained in New York and served as replacements.

British regiments raised in the spring of 1778 included the 72nd, 73rd, 74th, 75th, 76th, 77th, 78th, 79th, 80th, 81st and 82nd, of which six were Highlanders, the 73rd, 74th, 76th, 77th, 78th, 81st. Another Highland regiment, the 84th, was raised in 1779. As the war continued, several additional regiments were organised and served in the West Indies.

These regiments were to have eight line companies, one grenadier and one light company. Each line company was composed of 100 privates, 6 NCOs, two drummers, two lieutenants and one captain. The flank companies had one captain, three lieutenants, 10 NCOs, two drummers, two pipers and 100 privates. The 71st and 84th each had two battalions.

British regiment, blue facings.
40mm Sash and Sabre.

Light Infantry

In August and September 1774, Howe organised a Light Infantry Camp at Sarum. Howe's drill was an expansion of General George Townshend's *Rules and Orders for the Discipline of the Light Infantry Companies in His Majesty's army in Ireland* published in 1772. Among the goals of the movements and evolutions was to quickly form fronts without the long and tedious wheeling of close order battalions. Townshend's training stipulated two-man files operating together, one firing while the other loaded, taught to utilise cover such as field fortifications, houses and other buildings. Howe adapted Townshend's instructions, intended for individual companies, expanding them to organise composite light infantry battalions composed of multiple companies. Howe specified three interval 'orders': 'order' requiring two feet separating the files, 'open order' requiring four feet separation and 'extended order' with 10 feet separating each of the light infantry files.

Howe also expanded the tactical doctrine to combine light infantry companies into composite battalions that could operate as independent units. The fundamentals of both Howe's exercise at Sarum in 1774 or the more simplified version published in 1778 were similar. They required that companies be formed in two ranks, with an 18 inch to 24 inch separation that could be expanded to four or 10 feet if needed. After the combination of the light companies into composite battalions in 1776, it is unclear how these battalions, which usually included eight to 10 companies, operated in the field. Although Howe developed a detailed set of instructions for individual light infantry companies there are no similar directions on coordinating the multiple companies on the battlefield. The large size of the light infantry battalions early in 1776 and 1777 prohibited them from manoeuvring as a single unit, particularly if they were deployed in extended order. In theory, a light infantry battalion of 400 men deployed in a two-rank, extended order formation would extend over so large an area that it would be impossible for a battalion commander to exert any effective control.

Descriptions of the actions of large light infantry battalions in battles, such as Brandywine, suggest that sub-units, typically divisions composed of two companies or

British converged light infantry battalion. Note the variety of leather helmets and round hats turned up on the side or back. 40mm Sash and Sabre.

British light infantry company. 28mm Old Glory.

British 71st Highlanders in brown overalls. 28mm Old Glory.

even individual companies, operated in a semi-independent manner. While individual companies attempted to remain in contact with neighbouring companies they advanced or retreated as necessary based on the orders of their company officers rather than under the overall direction of battalion commanders.

Aside from light infantry regiments, large regular foot regiments could also prove cumbersome to manoeuvre in close order or open order, across broken terrain. In these cases, British and Hessian regiments sometimes operated in wings of four companies. Witnesses to the Battle of Harlem Heights in September 1776 reported the involvement of two Highland regiments but only one battalion of the 42nd Highland was engaged. Given its large size, the battalion – by operating in two divisions – was mistaken as two separate units. If operating as a single unit, these large regiments would typically be formed in close order to ensure they remained within effective command and control.

British 17th Light Dragoons. 40mm Sash and Sabre.

British Cavalry

The 17th Light Dragoons were deployed to Boston in May 1775. The 16th Light Dragoons arrived in October 1776, serving only two years, while the 17th remained in America until the end of the war. Each regiment was composed of six troops, each initially made up of 47 officers and men. In early 1776, each troop was increased by 41 men. As part of this expansion, the 16th regiment designated 32 men from each troop to form a dismounted light infantry division. These men wore the regimental coat, with shortened tails, brown overalls and a Tarleton style helmet, while carrying a Pattern

1776 short carbine. Elements of the 17th Regiment served with Tarleton's Legion in the Southern Department but maintained their regimental uniform rather than adopt the green jacket of the Legion.

Artillery

The Royal Artillery was organised into a single regiment, made up of four battalions, each composed of eight companies, increased to 10 companies in 1779. Each company included five officers, four sergeants, four corporals, nine bombardiers, 18 gunners, two drummers and 73 matrosses. When on campaign, limber and supply wagons were either hired or impressed from local civilians, along with drivers who were hired from the local population. The number of horses required for each gun varied by calibre, with a 6pdr gun requiring four horses and a 3pdr gun or howitzer pulled by three horses. While light 3pdr guns or battalion guns were typically assigned to each regiment, British commanders in America combined guns and allocated two guns to each brigade. Heavier calibre guns, including 6pdr and 12pdr guns were usually kept in an army reserve and deployed on an ad hoc basis depending on the tactical situation.

British 6pdr artillery section. 40mm Sash and Sabre.

Table 11 British Forces, May 1780		
Location: New York		
Lieutenant General Knyphausen	**Unit**	**Strength**
British Units	Artillery	435
	17th Light Dragoons	265
	1st Guards	410
	2nd Guards	405
	17th Foot	370
	22nd Foot	387
	37th Foot	356
	38th Foot	412
	43rd Foot	335
	54th Foot	344
	57th Foot	392
	76th Foot	645
	80th Foot	595
	82nd Foot (4 companies)	328
	71st Highland Grenadier companies	150
	42nd Highland	594
Loyalist Units	2nd Btn. New Jersey Volunteers	123
	4th Btn. New Jersey Volunteers	149
	Loyal American Regiment	179
	3rd Btn. Delancey's Loyalist	222
	King's American Regiment	286
	Loyal New England Regiment	43
	Queen's Rangers	441
	Prince of Wales' Volunteers	320
	Volunteers of Ireland	414
German Units	Jaegers	689
	Von Bose Musketeers	506
	Von Lossburg Fusiliers	489
	Erbprinz Fusiliers	463
	Von Donop Musketeers	425
	Prinz Carl Musketeers	515
	Landgraf Musketeers	481
	Von Ditfurth Fusilier	591
	Von Bunau Garrison	596
	Von Mirbach Musketeers	492
	1st Anspach Musketeers	514
	2nd Anspach Musketeers	487
	Von Knyphausen Fusilier	450
	Hessian Artillery	318
Location: Halifax	70th Foot	381
	2/84th Highland (5 companies)	322
	Royal Fencible American Loyalist	187
	Loyal Nova Scotia Volunteers	58
	King's Orange Rangers	120
	Von Seitz Garrison Regiment	344

Location: Penobscot Bay	74th Foot	455
	82nd Foot (4 companies)	300
Location: Canada	8th Foot	400
	29th Foot	400
	31st Foot	400
	34th Foot	400
	47th Foot (2 companies)	100
	53rd Foot (6 companies)	300
	1/84th Highland	400
Loyalist Units	Butler's Rangers	300
	1/Royal Regiment of New York	500
	2/Royal Regiment of New York	500
German Units	Von Ehenkroook's (Brunswick)	550
	Von Barner (Brunswick)	500
	Prince Frederick (Brunswick)	500
	Hesse Hanau Infantry	120
	Hesse Hanau Chasseurs	350
	Anhalt-Zerbst Infantry	600
Location: South Carolina		
General Sir Henry Clinton		
British Units	Royal Artillery	200
	1st Grenadiers	550
	2nd Grenadiers	505
	1st Light Infantry	620
	2nd Light Infantry	610
	7th Foot	463
	23rd Fusiliers	469
	33rd Foot	448
	63rd Foot	453
	64th Foot	442
	17th Light Dragoons	40
	British Legion Cavalry	200
Loyalist Units	Ferguson's Corps	100
	New York Volunteers	200
	South Carolina Royalists	200
German Units	Jaegers	274
	Graff Grenadiers	437
	Lengercke Grenadiers	387
	Linsing Grenadiers	348
	Minnegerode Grenadiers	349
	Huyn Garrison Regiment	409
	2/71st Highland	200

By 1780 the British army was still largely composed of British foot and German regiments, but the Loyalist and militia units represented a significant component.

British Tactical Doctrine

By 1776 the British army was guided by a new tactical doctrine. The 1764 drill manual stipulated a foot battalion, minus the light infantry and grenadier companies, was to be organised into 16 equal platoons, formed into three ranks, close order formations, with less than 12 inches between files. When the regiment was stationary, the front rank knelt to allow all three ranks to fire. When advancing only the first two ranks were capable of firing. Firing was organised by company or paired companies, referred to as 'grand divisions.' The experience of the Seven Years War taught that the third rank provided support to the regiment if threatened by cavalry.

After his appointment in 1775, Howe, having overseen the 1774 light infantry camp and experienced warfare in North America during the French and Indian War, revised the regulations. Howe ordered each battalion to operate in two lines and adopt open order, allowing for a 24 inch separation between files. He also instructed them to manoeuvre from the centre rather than from either flank. Howe recognised that the broken ground of North America required more flexible formations and the lack of significant enemy cavalry negated the need for the third rank. The battalion needed to manoeuvre over broken ground, across fences or walls and through heavily wooded sections. The withdrawal of the British army to Halifax in spring 1776 gave Howe the opportunity to drill the regular regiments in the new tactics. Howe also reorganised his army by establishing a formal brigade structure, commanded by a brigadier general or major general, with its own staff. In February 1776 Howe modified his instructions to reduce the spacing for the open order formation to 18 inches.

After the debacle at Bunker Hill, Howe, who personally experienced the British assault, stressed to his troops the necessity of reliance on shock tactics and the use of the bayonet. British tactical doctrine sought to limit British infantry engaging in protracted firefights with enemy units. Rather, after one or two volleys it was expected that British infantry would use the bayonet to drive the enemy from the battlefield. Despite this emphasis on the bayonet, the 1764 Regulations did not provide specific instructions on the use of the bayonet other than stipulating the first rank should level their muskets while the following lines should keep their muskets vertical.

British composite grenadier battalion. 28mm Old Glory.

Throughout the war both grenadier and light infantry companies formed composite battalions. During the campaigns of 1776 and 1777 two composite battalions of both grenadiers and light infantry were created.

With the introduction of the new formation, British commanders had a wider range of tactical options. While the two-rank, open order formation would generally characterise British deployments throughout the war, British commanders adopted a range of formations. Depending on the situation British units could contract or expand their frontage by forming in closed or extended formations. In addition, British units would be ordered to form into a three or even four rank formations when necessary. In at least one instance a depleted British regiment was ordered to form a single rank to cover a wider frontage.

When deployed in a two-rank line, each eight company regiment was divided into two wings, each of four companies. Within each wing there were two grand divisions of two companies. The companies themselves were generally referred to as subdivisions, each composed of two platoons. On the battlefield the regiment was the fundamental tactical formation, grouped into brigades. Common practice was to deploy a front line, a second line and then a reserve in a third line. Light troops could either be deployed on either flank or as part of the first line. Similarly, cavalry units could be placed on the flanks or in the reserve line to exploit any breakthroughs. Artillery was typically deployed in advance of the first line or parcelled out along the lines.

While Howe stipulated a two-rank, extended order formation in 1776, throughout the war British commanders adapted their tactical formations to the unique characteristics and limitation of individual battlefields. Criticism of the looser British formations began early in the war.

British brigade deployed for battle advancing against American positions.

British dismounted 16th Light Dragoons supporting a 6pdr artillery section. 40mm Sash and Sabre.

Actual battlefield experience led some officers to question the utility of the two-rank open order formation. While the open order formation facilitated movement over open ground and the two-rank formation allowed for greater firepower, the formation also resulted in a lack of tactical punch, particularly during a bayonet charge. It was felt that the looser formations negated the shock of the bayonet and that a two-rank line must be in close order to ensure success. Lieutenant General Clinton raised concerns about the open order formation soon after arriving at Boston in 1775, writing it 'was one long straggling line two deep'. In his post-war memoirs, Colonel Tarleton claimed the looser formations were the cause of this defeat at Cowpens in January 1781.

In April 1781, Major General Phillips deployed his forces in three lines at Westover Virginia. He stipulated that the second line, composed of the 80th and 76th Regiments, were to be deployed in a compact, three-rank line. Some commanders delineated various tactical formations for different situations. Major Patrick Ferguson directed his men adopt a close order for the charge, at 'common' order with an arm's length separation for firing and the wider open order for manoeuvring.

Loyalist and Provincial Forces

One of the biggest challenges to the British strategy to secure control over the American colonies was their ability to establish military units composed of colonists loyal to the British Crown. Throughout the course of the war, British officials – encouraged by overoptimistic assessments from Royal officials in the colonies – overestimated the depth of Loyalist sentiment leading to the development of unrealistic and flawed strategic plans. Despite some limited success, the lack of sustained Loyalist response was a major contributor to the British defeat.

British Loyalist Regiment De Lancey. Note distinctive white round hats turned up on one side. 40mm Sash and Sabre.

There were several types of Loyalist military units established by the British. Loyalist militia units were organised to maintain order in areas under British military control. These units were not taken into the Provincial Establishment and like American militia, organised themselves around towns or districts. They typically did not have a standard uniform.

As British military fortunes waxed and waned, militia recruitment followed. The recruitment of militia units was most successful when the regular British military forces established a strong presence and suppressed Patriot sentiments. Once the British army left the area, most British militia units typically dissolved in the face of resurgent Patriot activity.

The primary Loyalist formations were Provincial units modelled after regular British regiments. They were trained, armed and uniformed in accordance with standard

Queen's Rangers with a light infantry company. 28mm Old Glory.

regulations. These units were also organised along the British model, with eight centre companies along with a light infantry and grenadier company.

At the beginning of the war, British command was divided between Canada and American colonies along with the Atlantic provinces of Canada. Included within the larger American command area were Canadian Atlantic provinces, Newfoundland and Nova Scotia along with West Florida which tended to operate as semi-autonomous commands. In addition, some Loyalist units served in Bermuda and the West Indies.

Provincial ranger units were composed of a mix cavalry and infantry, similar to American legions. The Queen's Rangers included a troop of dragoons and hussars as well as companies of infantry armed with rifles and muskets and a company of Highlanders.

While most Loyalist units failed to recruit their full strength, some recruiting efforts were successful enough to expand their units into multiple battalions. The East Florida Rangers, Johnson's Royal Regiment of New York, the King's Orange Rangers, Maryland Loyalists, North Carolina Highlanders, Prince of Wales American Regiment, Royal North Carolina Regiment and the Volunteers of Ireland exceeded their paper strength, recruiting over 600 men. De Lancey's Brigade was composed of three battalions, totalling over 1,700 men and the New Jersey Volunteers, Skinner's Greens, expanded to six battalions.

During the course of the war, some smaller Loyalist units were merged with other Loyalist regiments and many Loyalist regiments recruited Patriot prisoners of war to fill out their ranks. Despite appreciating the role Loyalist units played throughout the war, there was tension between the leadership of regular British units and the Loyalists throughout the war. The British complained about the unreliability and poor training of the Loyalist units while the Loyalists objected that the British were overbearing and condescending.

The 'American Establishment' was the amalgamation of existing British Provincial regiments under a single military organisation in May 1779. These regiments included the Queen's Rangers, Volunteers of Ireland, New York Volunteers, King's American Regiment and the British Legion.

De Lancey's Loyalist Regiment. 28mm Old Glory.

Volunteers of Ireland Loyalist Regiment. 40mm Sash and Sabre.

These regiments were re-numbered as the 1st through 5th American Regiments. This action was intended to encourage Loyalist recruitment by elevating these regiments to the same status as British regular regiments. At the end of the war several of these regiments were placed on either the British or Irish regular establishment, while two were disbanded.

Loyalist units were issued arms and equipment of earlier patterns. Some units were issued the Long Land Pattern Brown Bess, while some arrived with wooden ramrods which had long been replaced by metal versions. As the war continued, larger units were able to draw stocks from existing stores.

While a listing of all Loyalist units would be unworkable in this guide, provided below is a list of selected Loyalist units, noting the year of their creation and some information about their organisation, strength, uniforms and service record where available:

Queen's Rangers Loyalist Regiment with Highland Company. 28mm Old Glory.

- American Legion: 1780: Three cavalry troops and one infantry company.

- American Volunteers: 1779: Raised by Major Patrick Ferguson. Served at Charleston in 1780 and virtually destroyed at King's Mountain. Green jackets.

- Black Company of Pioneers: 1777: Merged into Guides and Pioneers 1778.

- British Legion: 1778: Taken into British Establishment as 5th American Regiment. Initially composed of three troops of cavalry but expanded in 1780 to include six troops of cavalry and two companies of infantry.

- Butler's Rangers: 1777: Originally with six companies, growing to 10 companies with two light artillery.

- Bucks County Dragoons: 1778: Attached to the Queen's Rangers for 1779 and British Legion for 1780 campaign.

- De Lancey's Brigade: 1776: Three battalions, each of 500 men

- East Florida Rangers: 1779: Four Troops.

- Emmerich's Chasseurs: 1776: Two troops of cavalry and three companies of light infantry, one armed with rifles.

- Guides and Pioneers: 1776: attached to Loyal American Regiment.

- Johnson's Royal Greens: 1776: 2nd Battalion raised in 1780.

- King's American Dragoons: 1781: Formed from several independent cavalry troops.

- King's American Regiment: 1776: Taken into British Establishment as 4th American Regiment

- King's Orange Rangers: 1776: Mounted rifle company, served with Volunteers of Ireland in 1780.

- King's Loyal Americans: 1777: Part of Burgoyne's army, returned to Canada after surrender. Issued blue coats with white facings in 1778 but reissued green with red faced coats in 1780.

- Loyal American Rangers: 1780: Six companies, served in Jamaica and Pensacola 1781.

- Loyal American Regiment: 1776: Raised in New York. Green coats, later red, faced buff and/or green.

- Maryland Loyalists: 1777: Authorised for eight companies of 60 men each. Sent to Jamaica then to Pensacola.

- North Carolina Loyalists: 1780: Authorised strength of 611. Unit sent kilts from 71st Highlander's stores.

- North Carolina Volunteers: 1779: 257 men in 10 companies. Also known as Royal North Carolina Volunteers.

- New Jersey Volunteers: 1776: Also known as Skinner's Greens. Recruited six battalions but unit was reduced to three by 1780. Battalions composed of variable number of companies.

- New York Volunteers: 1776: Placed on the American Establishment as 3rd American Regiment in 1779.

- Philadelphia Light Dragoons: 1777: Two troops, Attached to the Queen's Rangers and British Legion before being merged with King's American Dragoons in 1782.

- Pennsylvania Loyalists: 1777: Authorised to have three battalions, the 2nd battalion to be composed of natives of Ireland and 3rd battalion from Catholics. Merged and served with Maryland Loyalists in 1779.

- Prince of Wales American Volunteers: 1777: 560 men in 10 companies.

- Provincial Light Battalion: Consistent with British practice light infantry companies were organised into composite battalions. The battalion formed from Loyalist units in northern and southern theatres. Companies retained regimental uniforms.

- Queen's Rangers: 1776: The Rangers were organised with eight musketeer companies, along with a grenadier and light infantry company. Later additions increased the unit to include a highland company dressed in kilts and then transformed into a Legion, by adding a hussar troop in 1778 and three troops of light cavalry in 1780.

- Queen's Loyal Virginia Regiment: 1776: Merged with Queen's Rangers.

- Royal Highland Emigrants: 1775: Two battalions, 10 companies totalling 610 men each, authorised to be raised from Highlanders settled in North America. Both battalions served in Canada and in 1778 brought into the British establishment as the 84th Regiment.

- Roman Catholic Volunteers: 1777: 212 men in four companies. Merged with Volunteers of Ireland in 1778.

- South Carolina Royalists: 1778: Four companies of infantry and two troops of rifle armed dragoons. Many Black people served in ranks.

- Volunteers of Ireland: 1778: Taken into the American Establishment in 1779 as the 2nd American Regiment in 1779.

- West Jersey Cavalry: 1778: Merged into King's American Dragoons in 1781.

- West Jersey Volunteers: 1778: Merged into New Jersey Volunteers.

German Organisation and Training

With the beginning of hostilities in 1775, the British government sought to secure the use of foreign troops to supplement their forces in North America. After tentative negotiations with Catherine the Great of Russia for the use of 20,000 Russian troops collapsed, the British completed agreements with several German principalities. Britain had previous experience using hired German troops earlier in the eighteenth century. 12,000 Hessians were employed by King George II in 1745 to help put down the Jacobite Rebellion and 6,000 Hessians supported British troops in Flanders during the War of Austrian Succession.

Loyalist artillery section. 40mm Sash and Sabre.

Approximately 30,000 German troops served in North America during the course of the war, drawn principally from the Landgraviate of Hesse-Cassel, resulting in the generic use of the name 'Hessian'. Additional troops were drawn from six other German principalities.

Table 12		Strength
Hesse Cassel - 1776		18,970
	Musketeer Regiments	
	Von Donop	
	Lieb	
	von Mirbach	
	Prinz Karl	
	von Turnbach	
	von Wutgenau	
	Fusiler Regiments	
	von Lossburg	
	von Ditfurth	
	Erbprinz	
	von Knyphausen	
	Garrison Regiments	
	von Bunau	
	von Huyn	
	von Stein	
	von Wisswebach	
	Grenadier Battalions	
	von Linsingen	
	von Rall	
	von Block	

	von Minnigerode	
	von Koehler	
	Jagers	
	4 Companies	
	Artillery	
Brunswick - 1776		5,723
	Infantry Regiments	
	Prinz Friedrich	
	von Rhetz	
	von Riedesel	
	von Specht	
	Grenadier Battalion	
	von Breyman	
	Light Infantry Battalion	
	von Barner	
	Dragoon Regiment	
	Prinz Ludwig	
	Jager	
	1 company	
	Artillery	
Hesse Hanau- 1776		2,422
	Infantry Regiment	
	Hesse Hanau	
	Jagers (1777)	
	4 Companies	
	Light Infantry Free Corps (1781)	
	1 Jager Company/4 Chasseur Companies	
Anspach Beyreuth- 1777		
		2,353
	Infantry Regiments	
	1st Regiment	
	2nd Regiment	
	Jagers	
	3 Companies	
	Artillery	
	1 Company	
Waldeck -1776		1,225
	Infantry Regiments	
	3rd Regiment	
Anhalt Zerbst - 1778		1,152
	Infantry Regiment	
	6 Companies	
	Artillery	

Beginning in 1776 several different German principalities were engaged by the British to provide troops in their efforts to put down the American rebellion.

King George was also the Elector of Hanover, and these regiments were directly at his command. Rather than being deployed to North America, five Hanoverian battalions totalling 2,373 were sent to Gibraltar and Minorca in 1775 to relieve British troops for redeployment. Additional Hanoverian battalions were sent to augment the forces of the Crown and The Honourable East India Company in India later in the war.

German troops began arriving in New York during the summer of 1776, participating in the Battle of Long Island on 15 August.

The German troops were organised into specific regiments, complete with supporting artillery and standards. Although the German troops were provided from several different principalities, the organisation of these troops was very similar, based generally on the Prussian model. All battalions were composed of five companies, either musketeer or fusilier, and a grenadier company. At full strength, a regiment would total approximately 780 men, but most regiments fielded just over 600 men. In addition, Brunswick and Hesse-Hanau added a light infantry company to each battalion. The battalions were organised around four equal divisions, each of four equal platoons.

The grenadier companies were typically organised into composite battalions of four companies each, totalling approximately 500 men. Table 9 includes the organisation of German units.

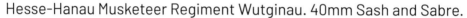

Hesse-Hanau Musketeer Regiment Wutginau. 40mm Sash and Sabre.

Hesse-Hanau Grenadier Regiment Von Block. Composed of the grenadier companies of the Wutginau, von Donop, von Trumbach and Prinz Carl regiments. 40mm Sash and Sabre

Several companies of German jägers also served in America. The jägers (German for hunters) were trained to operate as light troops, manoeuvring in a loose formation. The jägers were armed with a rifled musket, which had a greater range and was more accurate than the standard muskets, took longer to reload and did not include a bayonet. Instead, the jägers were armed with a small, straight sword called a *Hirshfanger*. Jäger companies were typically composed of four NCOs and 105 privates.

Hesse-Hanau Jägers. 40mm Sash and Sabre.

Jäger companies, including a mounted company, participated in all the major campaigns of the Revolution. Jäger companies were provided by Hesse-Cassel, Hesse-Hanau, Anspach-Bayreuth and Brunswick.

Three companies of artillery were also provided.

Keeping track of the names of German regiments can be confusing in that they typically took the name of their colonel with the exception of the Leib or Guard regiment. When a regiment's colonel was transferred or died, the unit took the name of the new commander. Over the course of the war many regiments changed names as their colonel also changed. The Anspach Regiment was originally designated von Voit but later became the 1st Anspach, while the 2nd Anspach was formally designated as Regiment Seybothen.

Although the German troops arrived in North America with a solid combat reputation, after the first several years of war the British became more critical of their reliability. While the jägers and grenadiers continued to prove their worth, the musketeer regiments and the garrison regiments were generally relegated to supportive roles. British diarists repeatedly noted that German regiments were slow to manoeuvre on the battlefield, tending to focus too much effort on regularly redressing their lines.

German officers took note of the British use of the two-rank line and while several regiments attempted to experiment with modified formation, requests to formally change doctrine were rejected by their sovereigns. While some units did evaluate the two-rank line formation, there were no attempts to adopt the open order formation.

Hesse-Hanau 6lb artillery section. 40mm Sash and Sabre.

French Organisation and Training

In 1778 France and the Continental Congress concluded the Treaty of Alliance, which formalised the relationship between France and the rebellious British colonies. Prior to the Treaty, France had supplied the Americans with substantial amounts of gunpowder and ammunition through a shadow corporation. The aid was channelled through the port of Saint Eustatius in the Dutch West Indies. American privateers and Continental warships used French ports to attack British merchant shipping. Although the French were sympathetic to the American cause, they remained reluctant to formally declare war against Britain. Although the American victory at Trenton buoyed hopes for a French alliance, the loss of Philadelphia in the summer of 1777 caused the French to hesitate. Burgoyne's surrender in October 1777 resulted in the King of France ordering that an alliance be negotiated.

During the course of the American Revolution, the organisation and uniforms of the French army went through some modifications. The two major expeditionary forces dispatched in 1778 and 1780 to assist the American cause reflected those changes.

French armed forces were organised into a Metropolitan army, Marine and Colonial forces.

The French Metropolitan army was reorganised in 1776 reducing the size of existing regiment from four battalions to two. The extra battalions were used to create new regiments. Each battalion included four fusilier companies, one chasseur and one grenadier company. Company size was increased and initially fusilier and chasseur companies were intended to have 116 privates. Most battalions struggled to reach their authorised strength and over the course of their involvement in American, French battalions averaged 500 men.

In 1774 the French marine forces were reorganised into 100 companies of a Corps Royal d'Infanterie de la Marine and three companies of Bombardiers de la Marine.

In 1772 the French Colonial forces in the West Indies and East Indies, under the command of the minister of the navy, were reorganised. Colonial regiments were largely recruited from local populations, with the officers coming from local gentry. At the start of the American Revolution there were 15 battalions of varying organisational

French Bourbonnais Regiment command group. 28mm Wargames Foundry.

structures, plus several independent companies defending French colonial possessions. By 1775 the West Indies regiments and the Isle-de-France regiment each had a battalion organisation of eight companies of fusiliers, one company of grenadiers and one company of chasseurs.

With the signing of the Alliance in February 1778, France declared war in March and the Comte d'Estaing sailed with a French army in April. D'Estaing's fleet, consisting of 12 ships of the line and 14 frigates, arrived in the summer. After rejecting an American proposal to attack New York, d'Estaing sailed to cooperate with American forces attacking Newport, Rhode Island. After the French fleet suffered damage from a skirmish with British ships and a severe storm at sea, d'Estaing withdrew to Boston for repairs, abandoning the Americans who were forced to abort the siege of Newport and retreat. The resulting recriminations between the Americans and French almost scuttled the new alliance but Washington was able to calm down the controversy, while d' Estaing retired to the West Indies.

D'Estaing returned to the American colonies in 1779 to assist American forces in besieging Savannah, Georgia.

France shipped to America over 200 artillery pieces and over 100,000 M1763 Charleville muskets.

In addition to the controversy over tactical doctrine in the years leading up to the revolution, the organisation and uniforms of the French army went through some modification.

D'Estaing commanded a composite task force composed of elements from different French regiments in the West Indies.

French regular army units included Agenois, Armagnac, Auxerrois, Canbresis, Champagne, Dillion, Fox, Gatinais, Hainault and Walsh. Artillery detachments came from the Artillery Regiment Metz while the force also included elements of the Belzunce Dragoon Regiment.

French Saintonge Regiment 1779. 40mm Triguard.

The units from the regular French army included regiments composed of two battalions of four fusilier companies along with one company of chasseurs and

French Saintonge Regiment at Yorktown, 1781. 28mm Wargames Foundry

one of grenadiers. The grenadier company had a strength of 111 officers and men while the fusiliers and chasseurs had 171 officers and men.

When deployed on the battlefield the chasseur companies formed a composite battalion that operated independently, screening the movement of the infantry regiment. Similarly, the grenadier companies were collected into composite battalions used as shock troops.

French composite chasseur battalion of four companies. 40mm Triguard.

Table 13 French Organisation		
	1776 French Battalion	1774 Marines Company
Headquarters Co.		
Colonel	1	
Lt. Colonel	1	
Major	1	
Assistant Major		
Sub Assistant Major		
Quartermaster	1	
Ensign	2	
Adjutant	1	
Surgeon Major	1	
Drum Major	1	
Armourer	1	
Chaplain	1	
Fusilier Companies	4	1
Captain	2	1
1st Lieutenant	4	2
2nd Lieutenant		
Fourrier		
Sergeant	5	6
Quartermaster Sgt	1	1
Corporal	10	6
Lance Corporal		6
Surgeon's Assistant	1	
Drummer	2	3
Privates	144	96
Grenadier Company	1	
Captain	2	
Lieutenants	4	
Second Lieutenants		
Fourrier		
Quartermaster Sgt	1	
Sgt Major	1	
Surgeon Assist	1	
Sergeant	4	
Corporal	8	
Lance Corporals		
Drummer	2	
Privates	84	
Chasseur Company	1	
Captain	2	
Lieutenants	4	
Second Lieutenants		
Fourrier		
Quartermaster Sgt	1	
Sgt Major	1	
Surgeon's Assistant	1	
Sergeant	4	
Corporal	8	
Lance Corporals		
Drummers	2	
Privates	84	

In 1776 the composition of French Metropolitan and Naval fusilier companies was different.

Also established were several colonial marine detachments from the Le Cap Guadeloupe, Martinique and Port au Prince regiments and Colonial artillery. These regiments were organised in a similar manner to the regular army regiments. They were not intended to be shipboard troops but since they were under the command of the Minister of Marine they were referred to as marines.

The colonial volunteers, composed of French citizens from the West Indies, contributed detachments from the Grenadier and Chasseurs of the Volunteers of San Domingo, Chasseurs de Guadeloupe, Chasseurs de Martinique, Chasseurs de Mole Saint Nickolas. The Volunteer Chasseurs of San Domingo were recruited from free black people of Santa Domingo.

Naval infantry, composed of infantry and gunners, were formed into companies and battalions assigned to ships of the fleet. While they operated as marines, they were referred to as naval infantry, and 359 infantry and 30 artillery served ashore at Savannah.

Approximately 500 sailors from the French navy served to man and supply the siege guns at Savannah. Table 14 provides an example of the eclectic organisation of the French expeditionary force that besieged Savannah in September 1779. D'Estaing's army included elements of metropolitan regiments and colonial units.

French composite grenadier battalion of four companies. 40mm Triguard.

Table 14 French Forces at Savannah, September 1779		
Comte d' Estaing		
	Unit	**Strength**
Noailles' Division: Colonel Vicomte de Noailles		
	Champagne	
	Chasseurs	95
	Auxerrois	
	Grenadiers	60
	Fusiliers	140
	Foix	
	Grenadiers	80
	Fusiliers	200
	Guadeloupe	
	Grenadiers	50
	Chasseurs	50
	Fusiliers	135
	Martinique	
	Chasseurs	50
	Fusiliers	30
D'Estaing's Division: Comte d'Estaing		
	Cambresis	
	Grenadiers	90
	Fusiliers	90
	Hainault	
	Grenadiers	80
	Fusiliers	200
	Agenois	
	Grenadiers	90
German Regiments	Gatinais	
	Chasseurs	90
	Le Cap	
	Chasseurs	50
	Fusiliers	80
	Port Au Prince	
	Chasseurs	50
	Fusiliers	30
	Volunteers of Valbel	80
	Metz Artillery	150
Dillon's Division: Comte Dillon		
	Armagnac	
	Grenadiers	50
	Chasseurs	50
	Fusiliers	175

	Dillon	
	Grenadiers	90
	Fusiliers	250
Independent Units	Grenadier Volunteers of San Domingo	156
	Dragoons	49
	Naval Infantry	359
	Naval Artillery	30
	Volunteer Chasseurs of San Domingo	545
	Chasseurs de Guadeloupe	25
	Chasseurs de Martinique	25
	Chasseurs de Mole St. Nicholas	25
	Sailors	500

The composition of Comte d'Estaing's 1779 expeditionary force that attacked Savannah included a mix of Metropolitan and Colonial formations.

In 1778 King Louis XVI authorised the Duc de Lauzun to form the *Volontaires Étrangers de la Marine* (Foreign Volunteers of the Navy). The Volontaires were intended for colonial service and were therefore under the administration of the Department of the Marine.

The Volontaires were to be composed of eight legions and a headquarters company. Each legion would include eight companies, including two fusilier companies, one of grenadiers and one of chasseurs, one artillery company, two hussar companies and an artificer company. Recruiting difficulties resulted in only three legions, numbers 1–3 being formed. Lauzun commanded a Legion sent to Senegal in late 1778, capturing Fort Saint Louis from the British in January 1779. Later in 1779, the Volunteers were amalgamated with the Volontaires Étrangers de Nassau.

Elements of the 1st Legion served with Comte d'Estaing at Savannah, Georgia in September 1779. After the cancellation of the proposed French and Spanish invasion of England in November 1779, Lauzun resumed command of a reorganised legion, composed of the former 2nd Legion and new recruits, named the Volontaires Étrangers de Lauzun. The new legion was composed of two fusilier companies, a single company each of grenadiers, chasseurs and artillery along with two cavalry companies. One cavalry company was hussars while the other was lancers. Although Lauzun's Legion was included in Comte de Rochambeau's army, dispatched to America in the spring of 1780, shortages of transport forced Lauzun to leave behind the two fusilier companies, taking just the grenadiers, chasseurs, artillery and cavalry, totalling 600 infantry and artillery and 200 cavalry.

By comparison to the French forces dispatched in 1779, the Comte de Rochambeau's 1780 army included only Metropolitan regiments and Lauzun's Legion.

Table 15		
French Forces at Newport, 1780		
Comte de Rochambeau		
	Unit	**Strength**
Major General Baron de Voimenil		
Brigade Bourbonnois	Bourbonnois	900
	Royal Deux Ponts	900
Brigade Soissonois	Soissonois	900
	Saintonge	900
Comte Lauzun	Lauzun's Legion	600
Colonel Aboville	Auxonne Artillery	600

The 1780 French expeditionary force that landed at Newport was composed primarily of Metropolitan regiments and Lauzun's Legion.

French Tactical Doctrine

Prior to the start of the American Revolution, in the aftermath of their experience in the Seven Years War, the French army was caught up in an acrimonious debate about tactical doctrine. Proponents of Frederick the Great's 'Prussian Order,' characterised by deployment into three-rank line formation, movement through cadenced step and rapid fire, were opposed by those supporting the traditional 'French Order,' which emphasised the column as the primary infantry formation. A commission of senior officers were empanelled to evaluate both approaches and their final recommendations guided changes to French tactical doctrine promulgated in 1776.

The Commission recommended the use of the column formation to assault strongpoints, clear an obstacle or pass through a defile but established the Prussian order as the standard formation for French forces. The departure of Minister Saint Germain, who had supported the revised doctrine, allowed the supporters of the French Order to reverse the recommendations of the Commission.

The issue came to a head in 1778 as the French were training for a possible invasion of England. With a large force of infantry and cavalry assembled in Normandy, a field exercise was organised to pit both systems against one another. The Prussian order forces were commanded by Rochambeau, who had also served on Saint Germain's commission. Rochambeau's forces consistently outmanoeuvred their opponents, conclusively settling the debate and resulting in Rochambeau being given command of the French expeditionary force, dispatched in 1780.

Another important improvement in the French army initiated by Saint Germain was implementation of reforms to the organisation and equipment of the artillery. Saint Germain supported the work of Jean Baptiste Gribeauval, who had commanded the Austrian artillery during the Seven Years War and was entrusted by Saint Germain with reorganising the French artillery. Gribeauval's plan reorganised the artillery around their intended battlefield roles. The heavy 24lb and 16lb guns were relegated to fortress defence and siege operations. The 12lb, 8lb and 4lb field guns were redesigned to incorporate lighter gun carriages featuring iron axletrees and larger diameter wheels. Howitzers were also introduced into the French artillery. In addition, stronger, lighter and waterproof ammunition wagons were developed and greater interchangeability of all parts from different arsenals was mandated.

Spanish Organisation and Training

The Spanish involvement in the American Revolution was not as straightforward as the French intervention. While the French reached an agreement with the American Continental Congress in 1778 and completed a direct alliance with the Americans, the Spanish supported the American cause largely through their alliance with the French and third-party suppliers.

In 1776 the Spanish claimed a large area west of the Mississippi River including the town of New Orleans. Spanish possessions were also scattered throughout the West Indies with the island of Cuba their largest single colony. The British occupied land east of the Mississippi along the Gulf of Mexico to Florida.

From the beginning of the conflict the French were deeply interested in securing an alliance with Spain to oppose Britain. Spain initially was sceptical that Britain's power would be significantly weakened by the loss of the American colonies and was suspicious of the creation of a republican nation on the doorstep of their North America Colonies. The French continued to propose an alliance with the Spanish and engaged in protracted negotiations in early 1777, trying to secure an agreement that the Spanish to jointly declare war against England in 1778. Although the French and Americans concluded a formal alliance in early 1778, the Spanish remained reluctant to do the same. Despite this, the Spanish secretly provided arms, ammunition and funds to the Americans in exchange for much-needed flour. That aid included over 200 cannons, 30,000 muskets and uniforms and over 300,000 pounds of gun powder. Spanish ambitions in their negotiations with France included reclaiming Gibraltar, East and West Florida as well as Jamaica.

While the French dispatched a large naval task force carrying French army units to America in July 1778, the Spanish refused American requests to deploy the bulk of their navy to attack British supply convoys. The French continued to negotiate an agreement with Spain for a joint invasion of England and the fleet was needed to support the attack.

In April 1779, an agreement was signed, the Treaty of Aranjuez, pledging France to support Spanish efforts to regain Gibraltar, East and West Florida and prohibiting Spain from concluding peace with England without French approval. Both agreed to a joint invasion of England. While the French assembled a large army in Normandy the invasion never materialised, much to the disappointment of the Spanish. Spanish attention then turned to efforts to recapture Gibraltar. The British successfully reinforced Gibraltar and despite continuing their efforts, Spain and their French allies remained unable to capture the fortress.

With their entry into the war in 1779, Spanish efforts in North America focused on British possessions in the West Indies and Florida. The Spanish captured Mobile after a two-week siege on 13 March 1780. When the British successfully reinforced Pensacola in April, the Spanish delayed their attack to assemble additional forces until October. Just after leaving Havana, the Spanish fleet was dispersed by a hurricane and the attack was delayed until March 1781. The siege lasted until 10 May when the British garrison surrendered. The result was the Spanish occupation of West Florida.

In 1781 Spanish authorities in Havana raised substantial funds in response to a plea from the Comte de Rochambeau to support the joint French and American attack on British forces at Yorktown.

Spanish infantry regiments were composed of two battalions of nine companies each. The battalions were composed of eight fusilier and one grenadier company.

Native Americans

While the main theatre of operations throughout the Revolution was centred on the eastern seaboard, the struggle between American colonists and Native American Indian tribes along the western frontier is often overlooked. The historical relationship between the European colonists and Native American nations was complex, although characterised by a continuing series of 'wars' as the colonists expanded their settlements and pushed further west. In addition to the establishment of permanent settlements by settlers, the colonists and Native Americans were engaged in competition in the lucrative trapping, trading and selling of furs.

The Proclamation of 1763, which ended the French and Indian War, reserved the lands west of the Appalachian Mountains for Native Americans. Despite this reservation, colonial settlers continued to expand their settlements over the Appalachian Mountains. Colonial governments chaffed under these limitations placed on expanding their territory, further inflaming colonial resentment.

The American Declaration of Independence, adopted in July 1776, included a series of charges against King George III. These charges included criticism of the limitations on westward expansion. More seriously, the Declaration charged that the British government had encouraged the Native American warriors to attack the Colonial settlements. British officials based in the network of forts and trading posts on the western frontier encouraged Indian warriors to raid settlements that supported the revolution, aided by Loyalists from those communities.

Despite close relations with the British authorities, most Indian tribes initially attempted to remain neutral. During the American invasion of Canada several tribes allied with the British.

The Iroquois Confederacy, composed of six Native American nations in New York, which largely allied itself with the British during the French and Indian War, was more divided during the Revolution. The Oneida and Tuscarora allied with the Americans while the others – Mohawks, Cayuga, Onodaga and Seneca – sided with the British.

In the Ohio Territory, the Delaware nation attempted to remain neutral but eventually sided with the British and continued to resist settler expansion for a decade after the end of the war in 1782.

In the south the conflict with Native American tribes was more pronounced, with low level warfare characterising the entire period. The Choctaws and Chickasaws allied with the British

The British abandoned their Native American allies after their defeat and despite concluding treaties with several nations, the new American government found it was impossible to stem the westward expansion of settlers into tribal lands.

Native American warriors were used as scouts, utilising skills learned from childhood to move stealthily through the forest and discover evidence of enemy movements through heightened senses of smell. During battle the warriors operated as light infantry in loose order formations. While they were effective in ambush or hit and run raids on poorly defended outposts, the warriors were typically unable to defend positions against formed troops. When attacking frontier forts or well-defended outposts, the Native American warriors needed the collaboration of British or Loyalists troops. Given their relatively small numbers, the Native tribes were sensitive to casualties and sometimes abandoned their British and Loyalist allies after minor reverses or the loss of significant warriors during a battle.

The largest contingent of Native Americans participated in the 1777 Canadian campaign. Lieutenant General Burgoyne employed over 300 warriors from eight different tribes while Colonel Saint Leger commanded over 1,000 from the Senecas, Tuscaroras, Mississagies and Mohawk tribes in a sweep down the Mohawk River Valley. Although the Native Americans suffered a large number of casualties and abandoned Burgoyne prior to his surrender in October 1777, the fighting between British-allied tribes, supported by Loyalist units and American settlements in New York and Pennsylvania, continued into 1778. The warfare was characterised by a deadly series of raids and counter raids.

In response to the devastation of frontier settlements in New York and Pennsylvania, General George Washington dispatched an expedition in 1779 into Iroquois territory to destroy villages and crops. Commanded by Major General Sullivan, the expedition destroyed 40 villages forcing Iroquois refugees to seek shelter with their British allies. The expedition ended with the Iroquois defeat at Newtown on 29 August. Despite these losses, raiding warbands reappeared in early 1780 followed by large-scale attacks which included regular British units. In September 1780 Sir John Johnson assembled a force of 750 men from the British 20th and 34th Regiments, along with Hessian jägers, Butler's Rangers and Mohawk warbands for an extended raid into the Mohawk Valley.

Further south along the Pennsylvania and Virginia frontier, the Delawares and Shawnees engaged in a series of raids until General George Rogers Clark captured southern Illinois, leading to the signing of a treaty with the Delawares, although the Shawnees continued to launch their raids into Virginia.

Relations between the settlers and tribes in the Carolinas remained tense throughout the war and in 1781, the Cherokees raided settlements in South Carolina. In response, General Pickens, commanding 400 mounted militia, destroyed 14 villages. Although major fighting with regular British forces ended in 1781 the conflict between the Americans and Indians continued. In 1782 Creek warriors attacked American units outside Savannah Georgia. Major General Wayne rallied his men and defeated the Indians, killing the Creek Chief, Guristersigo.

At the beginning of the Revolution, Indian warrior strength along the New York and Pennsylvania frontiers was estimated at approximately 15,000.

Iroquois Confederacy

Mohawk	100
Oneidas and Tuscaroras	400
Onodagas	230
Cayugas	220
Senacas	650

Western Iroquois

Wyandots	180

Algonquins

Ottowas	450
Chippewas	5,000
Mississagles	250
Pottawattamies	450
Miamies	300
Piankashaws	800
Monomonies	2,000
Shawnees	300
Delawares	600

Uniforms and Flags

American Uniforms

Of all the belligerents involved in the American Revolution, the uniforms of American forces present the most challenging to document. American military units included both militia and regulars. With the exception of Pennsylvania, each colony passed laws establishing militia units. Only New York and South Carolina stipulated a uniform for their militia units. In the other colonies the militia wore a wide variety of uniforms and despite some attempts at standardisation by individual colonies, no level of uniformity was achieved.

The units of the American Continental army underwent a series of reorganisations through the war, as various states sought to provide their regiments with uniforms. In addition, the American army relied on France and other allies to supply large quantities of uniforms. In the end the uniforms worn by individual American units varied widely,

1st Canadian Regiment wearing brown coats with white facings and hunting shirts, leading the American attack. The supporting unit wears blue coats, faced blue. 40mm Sash and Sabre.

dependent on the relative wealth of their home colony, the receipt of uniforms from outside sources and the vagaries of the inefficient American logistical system.

1775–1776

At the beginning of the conflict, as volunteer formations were organised by individual colonies, their appearance was determined largely by their commanding officers. Some of the militia units had a long pedigree while most others represented an ad hoc gathering of individual companies from villages or counties. These units could vary in size from a company to a full regiment. Uniforms from the early period ranged from the reuse of coats from the French and Indian War to units outfitted in uniforms similar to those used by European nations.

In some cases, larger formations were organised through the aggregation of individual companies, each with their own unique uniform. As time passed each colony asserted greater control over the organisation of their units and assumed greater responsibility for their uniforms.

American early war militia unit illustrating the wide variety of dress worn by these irregular units. 28mm Old Glory, Dixon and Wargames Foundry.

Only New York and South Carolina specified uniforms for their militia and although militia were expected to arm and equip themselves, many arrived without proper arms or equipment. The wide array of firearms that militia units possessed, ranging from rifles and muskets of varying age, to fowling pieces better suited to hunting, represented a logistical nightmare, solved in part by the militia using their own bullet moulds, which required that only lead be supplied.

In July 1775, the Continental Congress required that all men entering military service should come with a good firelock, bayonet, tomahawk or sword, cartridge box with 24 rounds, a powder horn with two pounds of powder, two pounds of lead and a knapsack. At the time there were two American armies; the forces assembled around Boston under General George Washington and a northern army focused on an invasion of Canada.

In June 1775, the Congress designated a Continental Quartermaster General, Major Thomas Mifflin, who was empowered to secure military clothing. In September Mifflin requested funds to purchase cloth for both Washington's army around Cambridge and the northern army engaged in Canada. Over the next several months different schemes were pursued to secure the necessary clothing.

General George Washington first recommended that linen hunting shirts be provided as the basic uniform, suggesting in July 1775, just after taking command of the forces at Boston, that a supply of 10,000 shirts would be helpful. In addition to providing relatively inexpensive uniforms, Washington also believed that common hunting shirts would also unite the various units and end what he termed '…provincial distinctions which lead to jealousy and dissatisfaction…' By September, Washington reported to the Continental Congress that a lack of suitable linen supplies rendered his proposal unrealistic.

In response to the lack of uniformity among their troops, in 1775 the Massachusetts Provincial Congress developed what would be known as the 'Bounty Coat'. This style of coat was short, straight buttoned, and constructed entirely with fabric of the same colour.

The summer of 1775 – extending into early 1776 – was a period of transition as each colony attempted to meet their obligations. It was only in June 1776 that Congress recommended that each colony provide a suit of clothes for their units. Although uniform standardisation was the goal it was still the responsibility of individual colonies to provide uniforms, resulting in continued variation. In November 1775, Washington ordered the commanders of the 27 infantry regiments to meet and agree on uniforms for their units.

Table 16 provides uniform information for the newly designated Continental regiments. While there is reliable information for most uniforms, little or no information is available for several others.

American Continental regiment in grey coats with green facings. 28mm Old Glory.

Table 16									
1776 Uniforms									
Continental Regiments	Coat	Collar	Cuffs	Turnbacks	Waistcoat	Breeches	Stockings	Headdress	Notes
1st Continental	■	■	■						Hunting Shirts
2nd Continental	■	■	■						
3rd Continental									
4th Continental	No data available								
5th Continental	No data available								
6th Continental	■	■	■	■	■			Round Hat	
7th Continental	■	■							Sailor's Coat
8th Continental	■	■	■						
9th Continental	■	■	■						
10th Continental	■								
11th Continental	■								Hunting Shirt
12th Continental	■	■	■	■	■				
13th Continental	■					■			
14th Continental	■	■	■				■		
15th Continental	■								
16th Continental	■							Buff hat	
17th Continental	■	■	■						
18th Continental						■		Brimmed felt hat trimmed white	
19th Continental									
20th Continental									
21st Continental	No data available								
22nd Continental	■	■	■						
23rd Continental	No data available								
24th Continental	No data available								
25th Continental	■								
26th Continental	■								
27th Continental	■	■	■						
Continental Artillery	■	■	■				■		

The 1776 Continental regiments were uniformed in a range of coat and facing colours. There is a lack of information for the uniform details of some Continental regiments.

Officers' Distinctions

In October 1776 Washington established rank insignia for officers and NCOs:

Commander-in-Chief: Light blue ribbon across breast between coat and waistcoat

Major Generals: Purple ribbon

Brigadier Generals: Pink ribbon

Aides-de-Camp: Green ribbon

Field Officers: Red or pink cockade

Captains: Yellow or buff cockade

Generally, the coats of the units of the American army varied in colour, and were mainly blue, brown and drab, although green and red coats were used. Most had some sort of facing colour used on a collar, cuffs and lapels, although some only on collar and cuffs but not lapels while others only on the collar.

American Continental regiment uniformed in brown coats with white facings and hunting shirts. 28mm Old Glory.

One distinctive feature of the effort to standardise uniform coats, as reflected in the Congressional directive issued to the American commissioners in France, was to shorten the skirts on the coats. Another distinction that is notable among uniforms between 1776 and 1778, particularly among officers, were pointed cuffs.

1777

For the 1777 campaign Congress further reorganised the Continental Army, creating 88 regiments assigned to each colony based on population along with 16 additional regiments and five 'extra' regiments that traced their lineage to 1776. Five regiments of artillery and four regiments of light dragoons were also created. Responsibility to clothe these troops was anticipated would be shared between Congress and the individual states. In addition to locally produced uniforms, the American army made use of captured British uniforms and the importation of uniforms from France.

In 1777 the Americans reissued captured uniforms from the British 8th, 21st, 47th, 53rd and 62nd Foot, replacing the facings and making other alternations, as necessary. The Continental Congress first ordered uniforms from France in early 1777, instructing their representatives to order 40,000 uniforms. The orders were placed in batches of 10,000 or less. One batch required coats in blue and brown with red facings, with white waistcoats and breeches. Another batch specified red linings, facings and collars while others required white linings.

American Continental regiment wearing brown coats faced blue and overalls of various colours. 28mm Old Glory.

In addition to a lack of standards for the colour of uniform coats and facings, the size of coats varied leading to a mismatch between the coats and men. In 1777 this problem was addressed by the Continental Clothier, General James Mease, who ordered that uniform coats be provided in three sizes and regimental tailors were to adjust the coats as necessary for individual soldiers.

American Continental regiment in blue coats faced red and a mix of breeches and trousers and striped overalls. 28mm Old Glory.

Since commissioned officers did not receive government issued uniforms, they were left to design coats that reflected their own particular taste. While the practice began early in the war when uniform conformity was virtually non-existent, even late in the war General Washington complained of the varying styles of officer uniforms. General officers tended to copy Washington's uniform of blue coat with buff facings, lining, waistcoat and breeches, although there were some variations. Revised guidelines in 1780 eliminated the sashes but added silver stars to the gold epaulettes. Major Generals were to wear a black and white feather in their hat while brigadier generals would wear a white feather. Staff officers could wear either the uniforms of their original regiments or a version of that of their commanding officer and all aides-de-camp wore a green feather.

1778

In October 1778 Washington held a lottery, drawing to determine which colour coat, blue or brown, would be distributed to state regiments. Blue coats were assigned to North Carolina, Maryland, New Jersey and New York. The brown coats were provided to Virginia, Delaware, Pennsylvania, Massachusetts and New Hampshire.

American Continental regiment in brown coats faced red. 28mm Old Glory.

The first instance of buttons with USA on them was in 1778. In 1778 Washington, who took an ongoing interest in uniform details, recommended a short jacket, similar to a sailor's sea jacket, with functional lapels, short collars and cuffs in different colours. He also recommended overalls rather than breeches.

Table 17 provides a summary of uniforms of the American army in 1778. While the 1777 reorganisation of the army, in which 88 regiments were assigned to individual states, is reflected in the list, in the case of Massachusetts, the regiments were not given numeric designations until 1779 and are referenced by their commander. It is assumed that a distribution of the French uniforms is reflected in some cases.

Table 17 1778 Uniforms

	Coat	Collar	Cuffs	Turnbacks	Waistcoat	Breeches	Stockings	Headdress	
Connecticut									
1st									small round hats
2nd									turned up on one side
3rd									
4th									yellow tape
5th									
6th									leather cap
7th									
8th									
Webb's Additional									
Rhode Island									
1st									
2nd									
1st State Regiment									
2nd State Regiment									Short sailors jacket
Massachusetts									
Bailey's Regiment									
Greaton's Regiment									
Putnam's Regiment									Brimmed felt hat trimmed white
Nixon's Regiment									
Alden's Regiment									
Jackson's Regiment									
Wesson's Regiment									
Marshall's Regiment									
Francis' Regiment									
Bradford's Regiment									Fur cap
Massachusetts Artillery									
New Hampshire									
1st New Hampshire									
2nd New Hampshire									round hat
3rd New Hampshire									
Pennsylvania									
1st									
2nd									leather jockey cap
3rd									leather jockey cap
4th									leather jockey cap
5th									leather jockey cap
6th									
7th									
8th									
9th									leather jockey cap
10th									small round hat
11th									small round hat
12th									small round hat

Regiment	Colors	Notes
Stewart's State Regiment		
New Jersey		
1st		
2nd		
3rd		
New York		
1st		
2nd		
3rd		
4th		leather jockey cap
5th		
Delaware		
1st		yellow tape
Virginia		
1st		
2nd		round broad rimmed hat
3rd		
4th		
5th		
6th		
7th		
8th		
9th		
10th		
11th		turned up hat
12th		
13th		
14th	Hunting Shirts	
15th		
1st State Regiment		caps
2nd State Regiment		caps
State Artillery Regiment		
Volunteer Cavalry		
North Carolina		
1st	hunting shirts	
2nd	hunting shirts	
3rd	hunting shirts	
4th	hunting shirts	
5th	hunting shirts	
6th	hunting shirts	
7th	hunting shirts	
8th	hunting shirts	
9th		
10th		
Maryland		
1st		
2nd		
3rd		
4th		

Regiment									Notes
5th									
6th									
7th									
South Carolina									
1st									Leather cap
2nd									Leather cap
3rd									
4th									
5th									
Additional Regiments									
Forman's									
Gist's									
Grayson's									
Hartley's									
Henley's									
Lee's									
Spencer's									
Warner's									
Webb's									
Malcolm's									
Patton's									
Rawling's									
Sherburne's									
Thurston's									
Jackson's									
German Regiment									
Canadian Regiments									
1st									Light infantry cap
2nd									
Continental Artillery									
1st									yellow tape
2nd									yellow tape
3rd									yellow tape
4th									yellow tape
Light Dragoons									
1st									Light cavalry helmet
2nd									Light cavalry helmet
3rd									Light cavalry helmet
4th									Light cavalry helmet
Legions									
Armand's									Light cavalry helmet
Lee's									Light cavalry helmet
Pulaski's									Light cavalry helmet
Washington's Guard									white tape

By 1778 greater supplies of uniforms from France were available to the American army. Despite the distribution of blue and brown coats there were still regiments in grey and red coats in addition to hunting shirts.

States continued to supplement the efforts of the Continental Congress to acquire uniforms through domestic production or purchase from France. As part of legislation required of militia drafts, Maryland, New Jersey and North Carolina provided clothing.

1779

Limited resources led the Americans to order additional uniforms from France in anticipation of the 1779 campaign. Infantry uniforms were to be blue with white, yellow or scarlet facings, white with blue facings, and green with white facings. Drummer and fifer uniforms were to be in reversed colours. It was anticipated that approximately 100,000 uniforms would be required.

In 1779, in an effort to standardise the Continental uniforms, regulations were published requiring a clothier general for each state and a regimental clothier. The regulations included a provision that going forward, overalls, wool for the winter and linen for the summer, should be issued. Uniforms were to consist of one coat with shortened skirts, one waistcoat and one pair of breeches. The lapels were to button over to provide greater warmth during inclement weather. The collars were to button down but designed to be turned up in cold and rainy weather.

In May 1779, a revised scheme for uniform allocations was adopted. The plan proposed all coats be blue with white lining and turnbacks. The facings were divided into four groups of states as follows:

New Hampshire, Massachusetts, Rhode Island, Connecticut: White facings

New York, New Jersey: Buff facings

Pennsylvania, Delaware, Maryland, Virginia: Red facings

North Carolina, South Carolina, Georgia: Blue facings with white laced buttonholes

American Continental regiment in blue faced yellow coats and hunting shirts. 28mm Old Glory.

The coat skirts were to extend to the mid-thigh, sleeves to have reinforced elbows and the coats be provided in three different sizes. Trumpeters, drummers and fifers were to be dressed in reversed facing colour, except those with blue facings, in which case the facings should be laced in white. Infantry were to be provided with a cocked hat, bound in white, while artillery hats were to be bound in yellow. The light dragoons were to wear leather caps with a green horsehair comb. Light infantry, drummers and fifers were also to wear leather caps. White breeches and overalls were to be worn by the infantry.

In October, continued shortages of adequate clothing stocks resulted in the Continental Board of War requesting that individual states assume responsibility for providing clothing for their regiments, consistent with the previously adopted regulations. Despite the adopted uniform plan, many units continued to wear older versions of their uniforms or were outfitted in brown coats. In addition, hunting shirts continued to be used to supplement the formal uniforms and in some cases were issued to replace worn out uniforms.

At the same time, American representatives in France continued to procure uniforms. A shipment of over 16,000 sets of coats, waistcoats and breeches arrived in early August, followed later in the month by additional French shipments. That same month, French and Spanish ships captured a large quantity of British uniforms including over 3,600 coats and related clothing. The British uniforms were dyed brown and later distributed to regiments from New Hampshire, New York and New Jersey in 1782.

American 3rd Light Dragoon Regiment. 28mm Old Glory.

1780

With the arrival of additional shipments of French uniforms, the 1779 uniform allocation continued to be implemented, although state governments played a bigger role in providing their regiments with appropriate clothing. In 1780 American regiments were still in the process of shortening their coats. Major General Anthony Wayne ordered his Pennsylvania regiments to shorten their coats in October 1780. Several months later Major General Lafayette ordered his light infantry to also shorten their coats in preparation for deployment to the Southern Department.

1781

Despite an estimate that approximately 29,000 new coats would be needed for the 1781 campaign season and continuing shortages, the Continental army that marched south from New York to besiege the British at Yorktown was reported by their French allies to be well uniformed. Conditions for the Continental units operating in the Southern Department under Major General Greene struggled to maintain adequate uniforms.

1782

With the surrender of the British Army at Yorktown in October 1781, active campaigning diminished. In the Northern and Middle Departments, British forces retired into their strongholds around New York. In the Southern Department British forces slowly contracted their chain of outposts, withdrawing into Charleston and Savannah. Ongoing uniform shortages for the Continental army resulted in a directive to use red facings for all new uniform coats despite the previous regulations. In addition, Washington advised regimental commanders to focus on consistency of style and colour of uniforms rather than adhering to the uniform requirements.

1783

Although uniform shortages continued after the end of hostilities the Continental Congress adopted a revised design for army uniforms. These regulations, adopted as the American Army continued to reduce in size, proposed specifications for coats and breeches and overalls and hunting shirts as part of the standard uniforms.

Light Infantry

Since the beginning of the war the American army included units designated as light infantry, ranging from a single company to a regiment. These units were consolidated at various times on an ad hoc basis for specific campaigns but never as a formal organisation. While these units were referred to as light infantry, they were not trained in formal light infantry tactics, but included rifle armed troops and usually operated as scouts or advance guards.

Washington organised light infantry formations during the 1777 Brandywine campaign after sending several veteran rifle regiments north to assist Major General Gates during the Saratoga campaign. In 1778, leading up to the battle of Monmouth, Washington formed units of 'picked men' to lead his pursuit of the British army after the evacuation of Philadelphia.

The 1779 Continental regimental reorganisation added a light infantry company to each regiment. These units were outfitted in the same manner as their parent regiments, although most wore leather helmets of varying design. As commander of the light infantry corps organised for the assault on Stony Point, Brigadier General Anthony Wayne requested new uniforms for the light infantry. Although Washington denied this request, Wayne did authorise the widespread use of leather caps with horsehair decorations.

After the successful action at Stony Point, the light infantry companies were returned to their parent regiments, but in 1780 Washington formally created a separate light infantry corps under the command of the Marquis de Lafayette. The newly formed Light Corps totalled 12 battalions of four companies. While the units retained their original uniforms, Lafayette added a red over black plume to their helmets. When

Lafayette's Light Infantry Corps 1781 wearing distinctive leather helmets with red over black plume. 28mm Old Glory.

Lafayette marched south in 1781 with three light infantry battalions, each carried a white silk flag bearing a laurel wreath and the mottos 'No Other' and *'Ultima Ratio'* (The final reckoning).

Legion Uniforms

The three legions, authorised by the 1778 Continental army reorganisation, were uniformed according to the preferences of their commanders. Pulaski's Legion wore dark blue coats with red facings while Armand's Legion wore similar blue jackets with buff facings.

Lee's Legion began wearing buff coats with green facings, buff waistcoats and brown leather breeches. McLane's light infantry company, which joined the legion in 1779, were outfitted in coats and overalls dyed purple and wore a leather cap with green turbans. When assigned to the Southern Department in late 1780 the entire unit was issued short green jacket coats.

Flags

Trying to comprehensively capture the wide range of standards and colours carried by American units during the course of the Revolution, particularly during the initial period, is as daunting as describing the uniforms they wore. From the beginning of the conflict the state and militia units that were assembled first at Cambridge and then concentrated into the formal Continental army carried with them colours of their own individual design, resulting in a wide variety of flags in different colours, sizes and designs. These early flags carried a plethora of images, including beehives, rattlesnakes, eagles, lions, bears, trees, Native American Indians and many other devices. Most of the early flags were made of silk with symbols either painted or embroidered and included a motto in either English or Latin. The infantry flag tended to be square in shape ranging in size from 18 inch cavalry standards to regimental colours seven feet square.

Even before efforts were made to standardise uniforms, some states developed schemes for colours. In 1775 the Connecticut General Assembly formed eight Provincial regiments. While uniforms were not stipulated, each regiment was allowed a coloured flag: 1st yellow, 2nd green, 3rd scarlet, 4th crimson, 5th white, 6th azure, 7th blue and 8th orange.

With the formation of the Continental regiments in 1776, each regiment was allocated two colours. In early 1776 Washington also stipulated that each regiment was to be issued two colours. One flag was to be the Union and the second was to be in the colour of the regimental facings, marked with the number of the regiment along with a motto. For example, the 24th Continental's regimental colours was buff with a red field, white thorn bush with a flesh-coloured hand extended to pluck it, accompanied by the motto 'He that touches me shall prick his fingers'.

In addition, four colours for the grand divisions, (a grand division was composed of two companies), were also provided. These colours were green, red, blue and yellow and emblazoned with the word 'Liberty'. This practice was carried forward in 1777 with the subsequent reorganisation of the Continental army without specific specifications.

When referring to the Union flag, this typically meant a standard with 13 red and white horizontal stripes with a blue canton in the upper corner next to the pole bearing the cross of Saint George and the saltire of Saint Andrew. Variations of this design usually included the red and white stripes with different symbols, such as rattlesnakes, in the centre.

The national standard for the Continental army was not defined until late in the war. The flag featuring 13 stars and stripes with a field of stars was originally intended to be used primarily by ships. Although not authorised, some American units did carry a version of the stars and stripes. A flag featuring red, white and blue stripes without stars was used in 1777.

In 1779 Washington concurred with a proposal from the Board of War for two colours, one the Standard of the United States and the other a regimental colour. The number of the regiment and name of the state would be located within the curve of a serpent. Baron von Steuben's 1779 *Blue Book*, which guided the training of Continental units, also recommended only two colours per regiment and specified the location of each flag with a deployed regiment. Along with the revisions to clothing for Continental units, in 1779 the associated regimental colours were also modified to match the proposed facing colours. These colours were expected to measure approximately five feet square. While the regimental colour design was straightforward, there was continuing confusion over the design of the national colour.

In early 1780, a plan was adopted to provide two colours, one the standard of the United States, the other a regimental colour in the facing colour. By November 1780, 11 new colours along with 42 new division colours had been collected at Philadelphia.

British Uniforms

The Royal Clothing Warrant of 1768 formed the basis for uniforms of the British army when the American Revolution began in 1775. While the Warrant provided a structure for the uniforms of the army, units on campaign regularly modified the patterns as needs required and regimental commanders had significant influence over the appearance of their men.

The infantry coats had round cuffs and lapels. Waistcoats were to be either white or buff and shoulder belts' colour were to be consistent with the waistcoat colour. The coats of drummers and fifers of Royal regiments were to be red with blue facings and white lace. Red faced regiments were to have white coats, with red facings, turnbacks, waistcoats and breeches. Other regiments had drummers and fifers in their facing colour, faced red. If their coats were white or buff their turnbacks were to be red, while the turnbacks of musicians of other regiments were to be the same as the facings of the rank and file. Drummers and fifers were to have bearskin caps with a silver front plate with the King's crest. Regimental numbers were to be on the back.

The three regiments designated as 'fusiliers', the 7th, 21st and 23rd, were authorised to wear bearskin caps, slightly smaller those of the grenadier bearskins, rather than the standard tricorne. On service in America, while some officers may have retained them, the regiments reverted to the tricorne.

During their time in Halifax, Howe and other regimental officers modified the regulation uniforms, cutting down the refulation coats and modifying the tricornes in several ways to provide more shade from the sun. Breeches were gradually replaced with overalls and light infantry companies adopted leather caps of various styles.

Sergeants wore a crimson sash with a centre stripe of the facing colour. Regiments with red facings had a white stripe.

Centre companies wore black tricorne hats, while grenadiers were to wear black bearskin caps with silver front plate decorated with the King's Arms. Centre company sergeant's hats were to be bound in silver while the corporal's and private's hats were to be bound in white tape, with a black cockade. Fusilier caps were black bearskins, similar to grenadier caps but not as tall. Cross belts were generally in the colour of the regimental small clothes, either white or buff. Soldiers carried a goatskin-covered knapsack, linen haversack and tin water flasks.

Grenadiers' coats had wings on each shoulder.

Light infantry uniforms included a cut down coat with shoulder wings, red waistcoats and short black gaiters. During the course of the war, light infantry companies wore a wide range of caps, most patterned after light cavalry helmets, while others were made of leather, or from cut down tricorns. Some had peaks at the front, others at the rear and some had horsehair crests. Officers and NCOs carried fusils. Over the course of the war many light infantry companies modified their uniforms to conform to the unique conditions of warfare in the American colonies. Cross belts were blackened.

While the 1768 Warrant regulated the uniforms of foot regiments, there were a variety of units whose uniforms included variations from those regulations. In 1777 all regiments of Burgoyne's army in Canada were ordered to cut down their coats, making them similar in style to light infantry coats. Fusilier bearskins were replaced by black felt round hats or slouch hats.

British 64th Regiment with black facings. 40mm Sash and Sabre.

British grenadiers under attack. Note several figures wear a crimson sash.
28mm Old Glory.

When the Brigade of Guards arrived on Staten Island, Howe ordered all lace be stripped from their uniforms, although the 1st battalion retained lace on their shoulder strap. Their hats were modified from the tricorne to be instead just turned up on one side. Breeches were replaced by trousers and half gaiters and backpacks replaced by blanket rolls. British Guards deployed to America wore a cut down regimental coat with lace removed. Facings were dark blue. Half gaiters over shoes and trousers in a range of colours were worn. Wide brimmed hats were adopted as the war continued. Light infantry companies wore cut down coats without shoulder wings and leather caps or round hats. Officers and NCOs carried fusils.

British composite grenadier battalion advancing. 40mm Sash and Sabre and Triguard.

British light infantry company.
28mm Old Glory

Highland regiments wore red coats with white turnbacks and waistcoats in different facing colours. Although issued kilts of the 'government tartan,' the Highland regiments exchanged the kilts for overall trousers soon after arriving in North America. Highlanders wore a Kilmarnock bonnet, with red, white and blue diced band and tuft on top.

British foot regiment in the Southern Department. Note the mix of trousers and overalls and round hats, some turned up on the side or at the back, in place of tricorne. 40mm Sash and Sabre.

Table 18									NCO			
British Uniforms	Coat	Collar	Cuffs	Lapels	Turnbacks	Waistcoat	Breeches	Gaiters	Sash	stripe	Officer Lace	Headdress
Guards												
1st												
2nd												
3rd												
Royal Regiments												
4th												
8th												
60th												
Fusiliers												
5th												
7th												
21st												
23rd												
Highland Regiments												
42nd								stockings				Bonnet
71st								stockings				Bonnet
74th								stockings				Bonnet
84th								stockings				Bonnet
Irish Regiments												
18th												
27th												
English Regiments												
3rd												
6th												
9th												
10th												
14th												
15th												
16th												
17th												
19th												
20th												
22nd												
24th												
26th												
28th												
29th												
30th												
31st												
33rd												
34th												

| 35th |
| 36th |
| 37th |
| 38th |
| 40th |
| 43rd |
| 44th |
| 45th |
| 46th |
| 47th |
| 49th |
| 50th |
| 52nd |
| 53rd |
| 54th |
| 55th |
| 57th |
| 59th |
| 60th |
| 62nd |
| 63rd |
| 64th |
| 65th |
| 70th |
| 76th |
| 80th |
| 82nd |

Notes: These uniform details reflect the unform worn on initial deployment. Over the course of various campaigns many units modified their hats, coats and breeches to adapt to the unique conditions of warfare in North America.

Officers' Uniforms

Officers were required to wear a coat of scarlet faced in the regimental colour. The coats were to have rounded cuffs. Buttons were to be stamped with regimental numbers. Waistcoats were to be plain, and a crimson sash was worn around the waist. Grenadier officers wore epaulettes on each shoulder while officers of battalion companies wore a single epaulette on the right shoulder. Sword hilts were to match the regimental buttons, either silver or gold. Tricorne hats could be bound in either gold or silver lace. Gorgets in either gold or silver, matching the buttons, were engraved with the King's Arms and regimental number. Grenadier officers carried a fusil and battalion commanders carried a spontoon. Early in the war the American tactic of targeting officers resulted in officers downplaying their rank, abandoning the gorget and replacing the spontoon with a fusil.

Cavalry

Two British cavalry regiments were deployed in North America, namely the 16th and 17th Light Dragoons. Both regiments wore a helmet with a red horsehair plume, a coloured turban, dark blue for the 16th and white for the 17th. The 16th's helmet included The Royal Crest on the front while the 17th had a skull and crossbones image. While the 16th's trumpeters wore red coats with blue facings and yellow lace, the trumpeters of the 17th wore reversed colours, that is, a white coat with red facings, waistcoat and pants and a cocked hat rather than a helmet. Members of the 17th Light Dragoons, which remained on active service in North America throughout the war, later adopted leather buckskin trousers and wore hunting shirts in the field.

Artillery

British artillery was uniformed in dark blue coats with red collars, cuffs, lapels and turnbacks. White waistcoats and breeches were also worn. Tricornes were worn by most artillery companies although companies assigned to Burgoyne's Canadian army in 1777 wore light infantry style helmets.

British 6pdr artillery section. 40mm Sash and Sabre.

Drums

Regimental drums were made of wood with a front painted in the facing colour with the regimental crest in the centre. The regimental number was also included under the crest. The top and bottom bands were painted red.

Flags

All British regiments carried two colours. The 1768 Clothing Warrant dictated the design of the Royal regiments and some senior regiments. Each colour included the regimental crest at the centre. Royal regiments had the king's cipher on dark blue flags with the Union in the upper left corner, while the other regiments included the specific regiment's badge or number.

The King's Colour for each regiment was the Union, with the regimental badge or number in the centre. The other colour was in the facing colour and included a distinctive regimental badge or regimental number. For flags with red or white facings the regimental flag had a red cross on a white field. Regiments with black facings carried a flag with the red cross on a black field with the Union in the upper left corner. The Guards Regiments reversed the usual pattern and the Regimental Colour was the Union with the King's Colour being plain crimson with a painted device on it.

The emblems and devices on the flags were painted and each flag had mixed gold and crimson tassels. Both colours measured six feet (1.8 metres) on the staff and six foot six inches (2 metres) on the fly and included a spear and finial on a nine foot 10 inch (three metres) staff.

British foot regiment in yellow facings. Regimental colour is in the facing colour. 28mm Old Glory.

British foot regiment in yellow facings serving in Southern Department, wearing round hats.

While each British regiment had a regimental colour and king's colour, it is doubtful that every regiment carried those colours into the field during the course of the war. Concern for the safety of the colours led some commanders to leave the colours behind when on campaign or in supply wagons if deploying for combat. However, there *are* several examples in which regimental colours were present during various battles.

Loyalist Uniforms

While newly formed Loyalist units were initially designated to wear green coats faced in a variety of facing colours, some units were originally dressed in red coats, provided by the British government. At the beginning of 1778, all Provincial units were to wear red coats with different facings, while several select units, such as Tarleton's British Legion and the Queen's Rangers, deliberately retained green coats. Some Provincial units purchased clothes and equipment from British regiments that had been transferred home. Other Provincial units remained clothed in green for a period until those uniforms wore out. Loyalist coats apparently bore buttonhole lace with interwoven coloured stripes.

40mm Triguard Queen's Rangers.

Units generally wore white breeches and vests except those with buff facings, in which case they wore buff breeches and vests. As war progressed, breeches were replaced by overalls in a variety of colours including buff and brown. Leather crossbelts were white consistent with regular British units while legion and ranger units wore black crossbelts.

Cocked and round hats edged in white were issued to Loyalist units. Later, wide brimmed hats were issued which could be turned up on the side or back. Light infantry companies and ranger units wore leather caps with devices painted on their peak front.

Corporals were identified by a white silk epaulette or looped knot on their right shoulder while sergeants had silver lace on their hats, plain white lace on their coats, a crimson waistcoat with an interwoven stripe of the unit facing colour and a short sword. The NCOs tended to carry muskets rather than halberds.

Officers' uniforms were of higher quality and included gorgets, buttons, lace and sword hilts in gold or silver according to regimental regulations. The officers also wore crimson sashes and like the NCOs carried fusils, a shorter version of the musket, rather than spontoons.

Table 19 Uniform

Loyalist Uniform	Coat	Collar	Cuffs	Turnbacks	Vest	Pants	Stockings	Officer Lace	Headress
American Legion									
American Volunteers									
British Legion									Leather Helmet
Bucks County Dragoons									
Butler's Ranger									Leather Cap
DeLancey's Brigade									White round hat one side turned up
East Florida Ranger									
Emmerich Chasseurs									
Guides and Pioneers									
Johnson's Royal Greens									
King's American Dragoons									Dragoon helmet
King's American Regiment									
King's Orange Rangers									
King's Loyal Americans									
Loyal American Rangers									
Loyal American Regiment									
North Carolina Loyalists									
North Carolina Volunteers									
Maryland Loyalists									
New Jersey Volunteer									
New York Volunteers									
Pennsylvania Loyalists									
Philadelphia Light Dragoons									
Prince of Wales American Volunteers									
Queens Rangers									Black caps with silver crescent
Royal Highland Emigrants					Issued tartan kilts, stockings				
South Carolina Royalists									
Volunteers of Ireland		Wide brandenberg buttonholes							Short leather helmet
West Jersey Cavalry									
West Jersey Volunteers									

Loyalist units wore primarily red or green coats, although facing colours varied.

German Uniforms

The typical German soldier wore a blue woollen coat with long tails and in most cases without a collar. The lining and turnback was often red. The coats had short lapels, although garrison regiments had no lapels. The lapels, cuffs and the left shoulder strap were in the facing colour with buttons that were pewter or brass. Musketeers and jägers wore black tricornes while grenadiers wore a variety of tall mitres with large, engraved plates in silver or brass on the front and cloth backs in the facing colour. Fusiliers wore a shorter version of the grenadier mitre.

The waistcoats and breeches were either white or pale yellow with black linen gaiters over the breeches, stockings and shoe tops. German soldiers carried their bayonets on a waistbelt along with a short sword. They also wore a large cartridge box with a plate showing their Prince's coat of arms and carried a large fur backpack.

German sergeants' uniforms featured silver lace and Sergeants carried a halberd. Officers' uniforms were more elaborate, featuring sashes of colours according to their Principality and large gorgets. The officers also carried spontoons.

German jäger units were similar to American rifle units, operating in loose formations and able to manoeuvre across broken battlefield landscapes. The jägers were dressed in green coats, faced red with red lining. The jägers carried a hunting rifle and were armed with a short sword.

German artillery wore tricornes trimmed with white tape, blue coats, red facings, and white or yellow breeches.

Hesse-Hanau Trumbach Musketeer Regiment. 40mm Sash and Sabre.

The list below provides selected information about each German contingents' contribution to the war, providing year of arrival, theatres of deployment and further uniforms details to supplement the uniform chart.

Anspach-Bayreuth (1777): Two regiments participated in major operations in the Northern and Southern Departments. One artillery section of two guns.

Anhalt-Zerbst (1778): Arrived in Quebec and deployed to New York in 1781. Organisation and uniforms followed the Austrian model rather than Prussian. Grenadiers wore bearskins with brass front plate with a cloth backing in red, edged yellow. Headdress in 1781 included cylindrical felt caps similar to British Queen's Rangers.

Hesse-Hanau (1776): Arrived in Quebec and served in Burgoyne's campaign. Infantry lapels and sleeves had Brandenburg lace. Grenadier mitres white metal with yellow cloth back and yellow and red plume. Officers wore silver and red sash. Free Corps included one rifle company of 160 men and four light infantry companies. Free Corps uniform had no lapels.

Brunswick (1776): The majority of the Prinz Friedrich Regiment was left at Fort Ticonderoga and returned to Canada after Burgoyne surrendered. Von Rhetz officers wore blue breeches and high riding boots. The jäger company operated with the light infantry regiment.

Waldeck (1776): The regiment was accompanied by two 3pdr cannon. Grenadiers wore a bearskin with no front plate with yellow cloth backing trimmed white with a white tassel.

Hesse-Cassel: The Leib Regiment's had white Brandenburg cuffs. Von Merbach's facings were trimmed white and those of the Prinz Carl Regiment were trimmed yellow. Garrison regiment uniforms had no lapels except Wissenbach Regiment. Von Wuthentau's Regiment had no lapels. Jägers wore brown leggings.

Hesse-Hanau Fusilier Regiment von Lossburg. 40mm Sash and Sabre.

Hessau-Hanau grenadier battalion. Note offices with spontoons. 28mm Old Glory.

Hesse-Hanau jägers deployed behind gabions. 28mm Old Glory.

Table 20

German Uniforms

Hesse Cassel - 1776

	Coat	Collar	Cuffs	Lapels	Turnbacks	Vest	Pants	Stockings	Sash	Officer Lace	Headress	Pompom
Musketeer Regiments												
von Donop												
Lieb												
von Mirbach												
Prinz Karl												
von Turmbach												
von Wutgenau												
Fusilier Regiments												
von Lossburg											Brass metal caps	
von Ditfurth											white metal caps	
Erbprinz											white metal caps	
von Knyphausen											Brass metal caps	
Garrison Regiments												
von Bunau												
von Huyn												
von Stein												
von Wissenbach												
Grenadier Battalions												
von Linsingen		Composed of Leib, Mirbach, 2nd and 3rd Bttn Guard grenadier companies										
von Rall											Brass grenadier miter	
von Block		Composed of Wutginau, Prinz Carl, Donop and Trumbach grenadier companies										
von Minnigerode		Composed of Erbprinz, Ditfurth, Lossberg and Knyphausen grenadier companies										
von Koehler		Composed of grenadier companies from four garrison regiments in regimental uniforms										
Jagers												
4 Companies												
Artillery												
3 Companies												

Brunswick - 1776												
Infantry Regiments												
Prinz Friedrich												
von Rhetz												
von Riedesel												
von Specht												
Grenadier Battalion												
von Breyman	Composed of one company from each of the above infantry regiments											
Light Infantry Battalion												
von Barner												
Dragoon Regiment												
Prinz Ludwig												
Jäger												
1 company												
Hesse Hanau- 1776												
Infantry Regiment												
Erbprinz												
Jäger (1777)												
3 Companies												
Light Infantry Free Corps (1781)												
1 Jager Co./4 Chasseur Co.												
Artillery												
1 Section												
Anspach Beyreuth- 1777												
Infantry Regiments												
1st Regiment												
2nd Regiment												
Jäger												
3 Companies												
Artillery												
1 Section												
Waldeck -1776												
Infantry Regiments												
3rd Regiment												
Artillery												
1 section												
Anhalt Zerbst - 1778												
Infantry Regiment												
2 Bttn's in 6 Companies												

Uniform details for German forces serving in North America.

Flags

Most German regiments carried two colours. One was the sovereign's colour and the other the regimental colour. The colours of Brunswick and Hesse-Cassel were similar to Prussian colours while the Ansbach-Bayreuth's were of white damask with a crowned cipher in the centre, surrounded by a laurel wreath.

Drums

German regiments carried brass drums usually featuring the monogram of the unit's sovereign. Drum hoops were painted in the facing colour with contrasting diagonal stripes.

French Uniforms – 1776

In the years leading up the American Revolution, French uniforms were becoming increasingly standardised. Whitish grey undyed wool was adopted as the universal colour of the coats for regular French units, while Irish and Swiss foreign regiments wore red and German regiments were dressed in blue. Comte Saint German promulgated new uniform regulations in 1776, modifying the standard French coat, shortening the tails and adding lapels. Facing colours were added to the lapels, cuffs, turnbacks and piping on shoulder straps and around pockets. The coat collar was usually of a different colour. The breeches and waistcoat were white. The white gaiters had no garter and buttoned to

French Dillon Regiment 1779. 40mm Triguard.

the breeches at the knee. During winter, black gaiters ended below the knee. The black cocked hat included a small white plume for fusiliers, red/white for grenadiers and white/green for chasseurs. A fatigue cap, the pokalem, was also introduced in the coat colour with piping and a *fleur-de-lis* on the front face in the coat lapel colour. French infantry carried a fur knapsack.

Officers were required to wear the same uniform as their men. Rank was indicated through a complex system of gold or silver epaulettes. Sword knots for all officers were gold, mixed with scarlet for Metropolitan regiments and facing colour for Colonial units. Officers wore a gilt gorge with silver badge with the king's arms at the centre when on duty.

Drummers in most regiments wore a blue livery coat with regimental facings, trimmed in lace, in the king's white-on-crimson livery. The lace was to edge the facings and each sleeve of the coat was to have seven bands of lace, equally spaced. Variations included red coats for the La Reine regiment and some foreign regiments.

The artillery uniform was a blue coat with blue collar, lapels, red cuffs, piping and turnbacks, blue shoulder straps piped red with yellow buttons. The uniform had a short white waistcoat, blue breeches and a black tricorne with white plume.

The 1774 reorganisation of the marine infantry included a blue coat with red collar and lapels, blue turnbacks and yellow buttons. The waistcoat and breeches were blue while the black tricorne was trimmed in yellow lace. White gaiters were worn in the summer and replaced in the winter by black. The marine artillery wore short bearskin caps with a brass plate and were assigned a blue coat with red collar, cuffs, lapels, turnbacks, waistcoat and breeches with yellow buttons.

Colonial uniforms were not stipulated by the French Ministry and remained relatively unchanged during the period of the American Revolution. The West Indies regiments had a blue coat with no lapels and turned down collar, cuffs and shoulder strap of the facing colour. The coat had white turnbacks and white metal buttons. Grenadiers wore fringed epaulettes in the regimental colour, and these were white for the chasseurs. The

Hesse-Hanau and British artillery section deployed. 28mm Sash and Sabre and Old Glory.

turnbacks featured cloth anchors in the facing colour. White waistcoat, breeches and gaiters were worn along with a black tricorne with white lace border and white cockade.

In the East Indies, the uniform coat was white with a turned down collar, cuffs and lapels in the regimental facing colour. Turnbacks were white and grenadiers wore a fringed epaulette in the facing colour while the chasseurs wore a red epaulette. White waistcoats, breeches and gaiters were worn while the black tricorne featured a white lace border and white cockade.

Colonial artillery companies in the West Indies wore blue coats with red turned down collar and turnbacks. The hat was laced yellow. The Indian companies had blue turnbacks, and a blue waistcoat and breeches.

In the West Indies, volunteer formations wore a variety of uniform as did the Indian Sepoy and volunteer units.

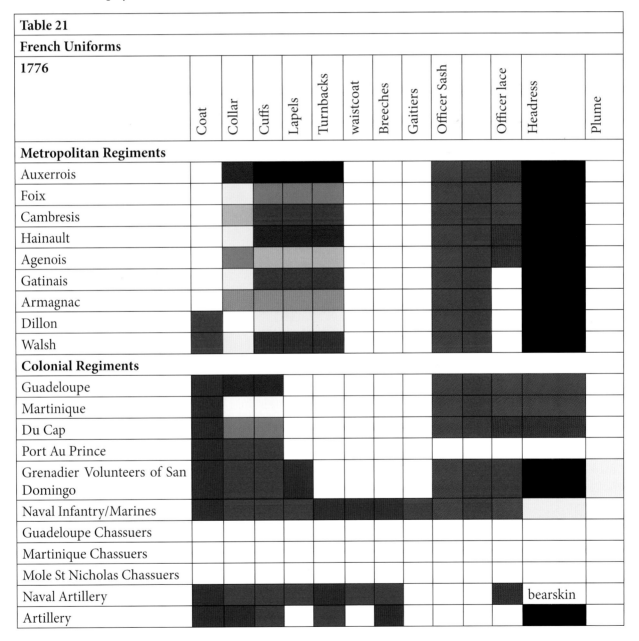

1776 French Uniform Distinctions

French grenadier battalion in column of attack. 40mm Triguard.

1779

The appointment of the Prince de Montberry as minister in late 1777 resulted in further changes in regulations. These new regulations saw the return of long-tailed white coats with white turnbacks, ornamented with *fleur-de-lis*, grenades or bugle horns in the facing colour for the fusilier, grenadier and chasseur companies. The revised uniform details were governed by the grouping of French regiments into 10 groups of six regiments, the exception being the Royal Regiment, regiments of the Princes and the Picardie Regiment. Each group was distinguished by a unique colour. Each group was then further divided into two sets of three. The first regiment had lapels and cuffs of the group colour. The second regiment had white cuffs and lapels piped in the group colour and the third cuffs of the group colour and white lapels piped in the group colour.

The lapels and cuffs were also white, piped with the facing colour. The collar was white piped with facing colour, as were the pockets flaps. Shoulder straps were white, piped in the facing colour for fusilier companies, green piped white for chasseurs and red piped white for grenadiers. The short plumes were removed from the tricorne other than for those grenadier companies that transitioned to the tricorne. In these cases the grenadiers were allowed a red tuft. White or black gaiters were stipulated along with white breeches. The pokalem was retained but the piping in facing colour was limited to the turned-up face.

The artillery retained the 1776 uniform but with a blue waistcoat and no plume in the tricorne.

It is difficult to determine to what extent the 1776 uniforms were issued before the revised regulations, completed in 1779, took effect. Another element of the 1776 regulations was the removal of bearskin caps from the grenadier companies. There is evidence that many companies ignored that order and kept their bearskins throughout the American Revolution. Prior to the 1776 regulations, French infantry wore a crested helmet and although the new regulations replaced the helmet with the tricorne, there is speculation that some helmets may have remained in service during this period.

To celebrate the American alliance, Rochambeau ordered a black cockade added to the traditional French white cockade. West Indies-raised regiments added a red cockade, reflecting the alliance with Spain, to their white cockade. A Dutch orange cockade was also added by French troops in the Dutch West Indies and the East Indies.

Table 22										
1780	Coat	Collar	Cuffs	Lapels	Turnbacks	waistcoat	Breeches	Gaitiers	Sash	
Metropolitan Regiments										
Bourbonnois										
Royal Deux-Ponts										
Soissonois										
Saintonge										
Agenois										
Gatinais										
Touraine										
Auxone and Metz Artillery										
Volunteers de la Marine										
Lauzun Legion Hussars										
Royal Infatry Marines										

French uniform regulations were modified in 1779 and it may be that the French units that landed at Newport in June 1780 were wearing a mix of the 1776 and 1779 uniforms.

Legions

The Volontaires Étrangers de la Marine were raised in France in 1778 and composed of foreigners, mostly Germans. This formation was initially intended to be made up of eight corps, although only three corps or legions were created. Each legion was composed of eight companies including one of grenadiers, one chasseur, two fusilier, one artillery, two hussar and one artificer company. The composition of companies was similar to the Metropolitan infantry with 144 privates in fusilier and chasseur companies and 84 in the grenadier company. The artillery section included four 4pdr guns, serviced by 171 men and officers. The hussar squadrons included six officers and 168 privates.

The 2nd corps, commanded by the Duc de Lauzun, was included in Rochambeau's task force, organised in France, and landed at Newport Rhode Island in 1780. Due to a lack of suitable cloth, the infantry uniforms consisted of a sky-blue coat with yellow facing, lined in grey. The epaulettes and standing collar were white, as were the waistcoat and breeches. Fusiliers and chasseurs wore a tricorne bordered in white tape while the grenadiers wore a bearskin without front plate. The artillery wore blue coats and breeches of the regular French artillery with yellow facings. Elements of the 1st Legion, which had been deployed to the West Indies earlier in the war, were included in d'Estaing's forces at Savannah in 1779. Infantry of the 1st Legion wore the same uniform but with a yellow collar.

The 2nd Legion hussars wore a sky-blue dolman, with blue collar, edged in yellow, and red breeches. Horse furniture, saddle cloth or shabraque, was light blue. Although issued a pelisse, it was not worn during the deployment to North America. One hussar troop was armed with lances while the other carried standard light cavalry sabres.

Senior Command

French generals wore a dark blue coat, with blue lining and cuffs, edged in gold braid, with two rows of gold braid on the cuffs and one on the collar. The waistcoat and breeches were white. The cocked hat was trimmed in gold braid. Staff officers also wore a dark blue coat with blue collar and cuffs. Waistcoat and breeches were scarlet, and the cocked hat was bound with a thin gold braid.

Colours

During this period, the French did not have a national flag per se, although a white one with a gold fleur-de-lis would be later adopted. Each regiment had a colonel's colour, a white flag with a spear point finial. Metropolitan and Colonial regiments had Ordnance Colour which featured a large white cross dividing the flag into four-quarters, with a unique design or coloured field for each quarter. Foreign Regiments featured different designs.

Spanish Uniforms

Spanish infantry wore a white uniform including a white waistcoat and breeches. Gaiters could be either white or black. The fusiliers wore a tricorne with red cockade while the grenadiers wore a black bearskin with a rear bag in the facing colour hanging to their shoulders but without a front plate. Sergeants typically carried spontoons. Officers wore cocked hats with either gold or silver lace and gold gorgets engraved with the royal crest. Drummers and fifers wore dark blue coats with scarlet facings and turnbacks. Their facings were edged in red and white lace.

The musicians of the regiments of the Queen wore reversed colours while Swiss regiments in Spanish service wore their colonel's livery. Drums were painted in either blue or in the facing colour and featured the regimental crest.

There were three units of Spanish cavalry deployed to North America including a squadron of carabiniers assembled at New Orleans in 1779. Two units of dragoons, the Dragoons of America and Dragoons of Mexico were also available.

Like their French, Dutch and British counterparts, the Spanish formed Colonial units in their overseas possessions in North America and the Caribbean. These units were of varying quality and intended to serve primarily as garrison units but also served alongside regular Spanish units. While many of the Colonial units were composed of both Europeans and Black men, some of these units had different uniforms for each race.

Spanish staff officers were distinguished by the pattern of gold lace on uniform cuffs. General officers were identified by additional gold lace on the collar, front edges of the coat and on the red waistcoat. Generals also wore sashes and red breeches.

Table 23							
1780	Coat	Collar	Cuffs	Turnbacks	waistcoat	Breeches	Gaitiers
Spanish Regulars							
Rey							
Soria							
Navarre							
Hibernia		none					
Aragon							
Espana							
Flanders							
Principe							
Guadalajara		none					
Colonial Units							
Habana							
Louisiana							
Voluntaires de Cataluna							
White Co.Santo Domingo Vol.							
Black Co. Santo Domingo Vol.							
Free Negroes of Hanava							

Spanish uniform details.

Native Americans

Most warriors shaved their heads, except for a short tuft which was allowed to grow about two inches long on the crown. In the centre of the tuft was a scalp lock, which was allowed to grow and was braided and passed through a small carved bone ornament. The warrior's head was dyed vermillion, a red orange hue. Vermillion was also a common colour used for ceremonial war paint along with charcoal, ochre and green. Warriors were also tattooed using a mixture of vermillion and charcoal.

Native American warriors wore a combination of native dress and European clothing. The Native dress included leggings and moccasins along with breechcloths and cloaks. Traditional colonial hunting shirts or European linen shirts were also worn, as well as parts of British and American uniforms. In addition to muskets provided primarily by their British or American allies the warriors carried knives and tomahawks. The warriors also carried war clubs carved from the roots of trees.

German regiment with two standards

5
Weapons of the Revolution

Muskets

The standard infantry weapon used by all the belligerents during the Revolution was the muzzle-loaded, smoothbore, flintlock musket. Soldiers carried a cartridge box holding 20 to 50 cartridges. The cartridges were paper tubes filled with black powder and a lead musket ball typically ranging from 0.6 to 0.75 calibre. To load, the soldier tore off the top of the paper cartridge with his teeth, and poured a pinch of powder into the pan of the musket on the lock. The remaining powder, ball and paper were placed into the muzzle and rammed down the barrel with a steel ramrod. The ramrod was removed, and the musket cocked to fire.

Brown Bess

The primary musket for the British army was the Land Pattern Musket, also known as the Brown Bess. In service for nearly 100 years, the Brown Bess included several different versions, including the Long Land Pattern, Short Land Pattern, India Pattern, New Land Pattern and Sea Service Musket.

Some regiments in America in 1776 were armed with the Brown Bess version issued in 1756, with a 46-inch barrel, while others were issued the 1768 version with a 42 inch barrel. Light infantry companies established in 1771 were issued the shorter version. In 1776, British grenadier companies were armed with a mix of the 1756 and 1768 versions, but efforts were made to standardise them with the longer 46 inch musket. Although the musket had a 0.75 calibre barrel, a smaller 0.6 calibre ball was used to allow for faster reloading.

The effective range of the Brown Bess was similar to that of all muskets. The musket was most effective within a range of less than 100 yards or closer. Firing accuracy dropped off dramatically at ranges over 100 yards.

The Brown Bess, which weighed 10.5 pounds, took 12 separate motions to load. An experienced soldier could load and fire five times in a minute while the average soldier could only fire two or three shots a minute. Since fixed bayonets hampered a soldier's

British light infantry carrying Brown Bess muskets

ability to ram the shot, many times powder and ball were loaded without ramming, which greatly reduced the effectiveness of the shot.

1776 Pattern Rifle

In January 1776, the British army ordered 1,000 of the M1776 Infantry Pattern Rifle based on a pattern by gunsmith William Grice. Grice's design was in turn based on German rifles, with a 30.5 inch grooved barrel, which extended the effective range out to 300 yards. These rifles were issued to British light infantry companies. 200 rifles were purchased from a manufacturer in Hannover while the remainder were manufactured by various British gunmakers.

Ferguson Rifle

Captain Patrick Ferguson of the 71st Highland Regiment invented a breech-loading rifle, receiving a patent in 1776. The rifle barrel was 89cm (35 inches) long and equipped with a sword bayonet. The Ferguson Rifle represented a revolutionary design which included an innovative firing mechanism that allowed the trigger guard to open the breach in one revolution rather than the 11 revolutions required by alternatives. This not only made reloading much faster but also made the rifle more accurate. Despite its increased effectiveness, the high cost of producing the complicated firing mechanism and limited reliability due to damage to the wooden stock, limited the practical use of the rifle.

Fusils and Carbines

Officers carried a fusil, a shorter and lighter version of the musket. Authorised for officers of fusilier regiments as well as grenadier and light infantry companies in 1770, by 1776 fusils were authorised for officers from Highland and Guards regiments. Unofficially the fusil was carried by most officers throughout the army when on campaign.

British cavalry carried a carbine, weighing just over 7 pounds with a 29 inch barrel and a pair of pistols.

40mm Sash and Sabre British dismounted 16th Light Dragoons armed with carbines.

Committee of Safety Muskets

The 'Committee of Safety muskets' refers to those muskets manufactured by American gunsmiths generally based on the design of the British Long Pattern musket, using new or reused parts. As the war continued, these gunsmiths shifted towards adopting French designs. Manufacturing of muskets was concentrated over time at various Continental arsenals located at Philadelphia, Carlisle, Lancaster, Head of Elk, Albany and Manchester. In 1780 Congress formed the Philadelphia Supply Agency which included the French Factory and Continental Armoury. Individual states also established gun factories. It is estimated that 80,000 muskets were produced by American gunsmiths.

Pennsylvania Rifles

American long rifles were produced by German gunsmiths in Pennsylvania based on the design of the German jäger rifles.

Rifles were flintlock muskets that had grooves carved inside a longer barrel that allowed the musket balls to spin when exiting the rifle. The spinning balls were much more accurate at long range. Americans had numerous long rifles that were accurate at 250 yards. However, rifles were very slow to reload. Soldiers often needed a minute or two to reload a rifle, since the grooves made it take longer to ram the ball to the breech. Rifles were often also built for hunting and were incapable of having a bayonet attached to them. While the rifles were effective at long range, the British learned that the slow rate of fire made the riflemen vulnerable to a quick counter charge.

It was not unusual for American companies to include a mix of musket and rifle armed troops. The lessons of 1776 taught that rifle armed troops were vulnerable to bayonet attack from British units. The slow rate of fire of the rifle made the rifleman vulnerable to a rapid advance from British infantry armed with bayonets. The American response was to closely support rifle units with musket-armed companies or to integrate the riflemen into the regimental formations. The limitations of troops armed with rifles also lead to calls from various officers to eliminate the rifle from combat units, when possible, but as late as 1781 several light infantry companies from Pennsylvania were armed with a mix of muskets and rifles.

28mm Old Glory American riflemen armed with Pennsylvania rifles.

German Musket

German troops carried a musket known as the Prussian Pattern Musket or Potsdam Musket. The 1740 version was a smoothbore musket with a 34 inch barrel and fired a 0.75 calibre ball. The musket weighed approximately 9 pounds.

Jäger Rifles

The German light infantry or jägers carried a hunting rifle, shorter than a typical musket, with a barrel length of 30 inches and a weight of approximately nine pounds. While the shorter barrel was easier to load and more adapted to skirmish combat, there was some loss of accuracy.

28mm Old Glory German jägers armed with jäger rifles.

Amusettes

German troops used several amusettes, particularly during the early years of the war. The amusette was a large musket, weighing about 50 pounds, with a 4.5 inch barrel which fired a ball weighing one pound, and were usually mounted in fortifications or on a light field carriage. The gun had an effective range of up to 600 yards. Although used primarily by German forces, the amusette was also used by Loyalist units.

28mm Loyalists firing an amusette.

French Muskets

The Charleville musket was a 0.69 calibre standard French infantry weapon, imported in large numbers to supply the Continental Army. While the Charleville musket went through several revisions, Americans were issued the Model 1763 and 1766 muskets. Shipments from France between February 1776 and May 1783 totalled 117,661 muskets, 2,125 carbines and 135 fusils. The 1766 version was somewhat lighter and turned out to be more rugged and reliable. The model 1777 was used by French troops rather than being exported to American troops.

The Charleville weighed 10 pounds with a 45 inch barrel.

Halberds

Halberds were usually carried by sergeants of musketeer companies and were used initially to reform the rank and file of a regiment during movement and combat. The halberds had a staff approximately six feet long. The iron head had a pointed spear tip with two additional blades set at right angles to the central axis. One of these blades resembled a hatchet head and the other was a sharp, downturned fluke or hook. The iron head could have elaborate contours and decorations.

Spontoon

Spontoons were also carried by officers. Spontoons, also referred to as espontoons, had a pointed iron head on a staff six to nine feet long, sometimes decorated with tassels. The weapon's distinguishing feature was a crossbar, either plain or elaborately ornamented, perpendicular to the main blade.

1st Maryland Regiment, 28mm Old Glory figures, including officer with spontoon.

Artillery

Artillery played a significant role in combat during the Revolution beginning with two 6pdr guns that covered the retreat of the British column after the raids on Lexington and Concord in 1775. Those guns scattered and drove off the swarms of militia harassing the British column, allowing them to safely retire into Boston.

A Treatise of Artillery published in 1756 by John Muller, Professor of Artillery and Fortifications at the Royal Academy became the standard guide for both British and American artillery officers.

Three types of artillery were used extensively during the Revolutionary War: field artillery, mortars and howitzers. The nature of the American battlefields limited the use of heavier calibre artillery due to its weight and lack of mobility. The use of heavy guns was restricted to set piece battles, usually sieges, around major cities or fortresses such as Boston, Savannah, Charleston and Yorktown. Standard siege guns included 9pdrs,12pdrs and 18pdrs, along with heavier guns taken from warships.

The most common field artillery consisted of 3pdr and 6pdr cannon, although both the British and Americans fielded 12pdr guns on occasion. A lighter version of the 3pdr, gun was used by the British, and German regiments were assigned 4pdr light guns. Heavier guns, 18pdrs and above, were deployed for siege operations or to defend fortifications.

American militia artillery with limber, 28mm Wargames Foundry and Front Rank figures.

Swivel guns were small cannon mounted on a swivelling stand or fork, allowing for a wide arc of movement. These guns usually fired grapeshot and small calibre round shot. Although swivel guns were usually mounted on sailing ships, they were light enough to be used by land forces usually on the walls of forts. In some instances, swivel guns were deployed in the field on solid bases, but their effectiveness is questionable.

Mortars were used primarily for siege operations. The British fielded several types of mortars including the Coehorn, with a 4.4 inch bore which could throw a shell 800 yards and could be moved by three men. The Royal Mortar had larger 5.5 inch calibre, firing a shell 1,000 yards.

Howitzers were also employed, allowing for plunging fire. The short barrel was fitted onto a standard artillery carriage and fired at a higher elevation than field guns. Both mortars and howitzers used hollow projectiles filled with explosives.

Artillery typically operated in two-gun sections served by a crew of 10 to 15 men for each gun. In 1781 the ammunition provided for each American 6pdr gun included 200 round shot, 30 rounds of grapeshot and 30 rounds of cannister. 3pdr guns were also assigned 200 round shot but only 20 rounds of grapeshot and cannister. Some cannon carried ammunition boxes on the carriage, usually on either side of the gun. These boxes could be removed when the gun was deployed for action. In addition, ammunition wagons were assigned to artillery units to provide additional rounds.

Cannon for both sides were cast in either bronze or iron. The American colonies were a major source of iron ore and by 1776 there were numerous foundries operating primarily in the north-eastern colonies. At the beginning of the war the American armies fielded a wide variety of gun types and calibres, reflecting the capture of British magazines and fortresses early in the conflict. American foundries began casting cannon with the opening of the war and by 1776 approximately 60 12pdr and 18pdr guns had been cast and shortly afterwards a standardised 4pdr light cannon was put into production.

Iron guns were stronger and could withstand larger charges of gunpowder, allowing them to fire the same projectile a longer distance than its bronze counterpart. Bronze guns were lighter and could be moved more easily around the battlefield. Bronze guns could also be recast while the iron guns were simply discarded when worn out. The French supplied 31 4pdr bronze guns of Swedish design which the Americans found useful. The French also provided additional 4pdr guns that the Americans found to be

40mm Sash and Sabre 40mm British 6pdr battery and officer.

overcast and too heavy for battlefield use. These guns were melted down and recast as three light 6pdr guns.

The field cannon fired a variety of ammunition depending on the tactical situation and range to the target. Iron cannon balls were used at longer ranges. At closer ranges grapeshot composed of a cluster of smaller iron balls housed in a bag was used. Grapeshot was also used by naval gunners to cut the rigging of enemy ships. At closest ranges cannister shot, a thin metal cylinder filled with either musket balls or iron balls were used. When fired, the outer cylinder shredded, allowing the balls to be ejected from the muzzle in an expanding cone pattern. Cannister shot ranges varied by calibre of the guns but were generally lethal with a 200–300 yard range. Artillery with trained crews could fire up to four times per minute.

In the Southern Department, two types of field carriages were used. The Galloper carriage could accommodate up to a light 6pdr gun. The carriage was combined with a limber so that a single horse could be used. Small ammunition lockers were attached to both sides of the gun. The other type of gun was the Grasshopper. The Grasshopper mounted up to a light 3pdr gun and featured two long tail pieces intended to absorb recoil and probably gave the gun its name. The gun could be traversed to a limited extent without moving the carriage. The gun could be transported on a horse in two pieces or carried on a wagon.

German 6pdr battery. 28mm Sash and Sabre Prussian Seven Years War figures.

British 40mm Sash and Sabre 3lb battery. Figures wear round hats rather than tricornes. The round hats were worn extensively by units serving in the southern states.

Artillery ranges varied depending on their calibre. Six pounder guns could fire out to 1,800 yards, although the effective range was 1,000. The broken nature of the American battlefields limited the use of heavier calibre guns. Most field artillery engaged with round shot at ranges of 600–800 yards. When the range shortened to 400 yards grapeshot was used and then cannister at shorter ranges.

While trained artillery crews were highly valued, the transport of guns was left to civilian contractors. Guns were moved by teams of horses on limbers. The use of civilians affected the reliability of artillery during battles. Once deployed on the battlefield the guns were manoeuvred by the gun crews. When the horses were withdrawn or killed, lighter artillery could be withdrawn by the crew manhandling the piece, although in the confusion of the battlefield these guns were abandoned on many occasions.

The list below, detailing the composition of artillery in the Continental army and Burgoyne's Canadian army in 1777 and Rochambeau's French army in 1780, illustrates the variety of cannon types and sizes used by both sides:

American Artillery 1777

Brigade Guns

Four guns allocated to 17 brigades

68 3pdr, 4pdr or 6pdr guns

Artillery Park

Two 24pdrs

Four 12pdrs

Four 8 inch howitzers

Eight 5.5 inch howitzers

10 3pdrs/4pdrs

10 6pdrs

Reserve

30 3pdrs, 4pdrs and 6pdrs

Two 12pdrs

One 24pdr

Battering Artillery – Cast in Iron

12 18pdrs

12 12pdrs

Two 5.5pdrs

12 8 inch, 9 inch or 10 inch mortars

Burgoyne's Artillery Train

26 6pdrs

24 4.4 inch mortars

17 3pdrs

16 24pdrs

12 5.5 inch mortars

10 12pdr heavy cannon

Eight 12pdr medium cannon

Six 8 inch howitzers

Six 5.5 inch howitzers

Six 8 inch mortars

Two 13 inch mortars

Two 10 inch mortars

One light 12pdr cannon

Rochambeau's Artillery 1780

French regiments from the West Indies were equipped with the older cannon that were part of the Valliere system. Rochambeau's artillery in 1780 represented the newer Gribeauval system. In the Gribeauval system, each regiment was accompanied by four 4pdr battalion guns. In addition to the regimental guns, Rochambeau's 1780 army also included:

Eight 12pdrs

Six 6 inch howitzers

Eight Swedish 4pdrs

Two 8 inch howitzers

Eight 16pdrs

Four 8 inch mortars

Eight 12 inch mortars

Two 8 inch howitzers

Fortifications and Fieldworks

Engineering was a specialised military art, and no less so during the Revolutionary War. The design and construction of field fortifications played a major role over the course of the war. Beginning with the British assault on American fortifications on Breeds and Bunker Hills. These field fortifications allowed the poorly trained American militia to withstand several British assaults.

At the start of the war the American army had no professionally trained engineers and relied on foreign born mercenaries. Despite a shortage of trained talent, American troops showed a proclivity for erecting effective fortifications to make up for their lack of military training and experience.

At White Plains in October 1776, the Continental army constructed an extensive line of fortifications to protect the strategically important village. British General Howe, a veteran, of the costly assault on American fieldworks on Breeds Hill, was reluctant to directly assault the American position. After several attempts to draw the Americans out of their positions and days of worsening weather, Howe retired south towards New York.

In December 1777, General Howe again attempted to manoeuvre Washington's army into a decisive battle. The British advanced from their fortifications around Philadelphia but found the American army positioned behind extensive fieldworks constructed along a ridgeline near Whitemarsh. Once again Howe choose to avoid a direct assault on the American positions and after several days retired to Philadelphia.

Forts played an important function in the American colonies, protecting important Atlantic ports and harbours and frontier settlements. Forts referred to a wide range of

American artillery deployed in a small redoubt. 28mm Old Glory figures.

types, including stockades, palisades and blockhouses. Depending on topographic and strategic factors, the design ranged from square, rectangular, pentagonal, hexagonal or star shaped.

The forts at major ports along the Atlantic Ocean were largely more sophisticated in design and oriented outwards towards the sea, which left them vulnerable from a landward assault without the construction of additional fortifications.

Large forts were built at military posts around the edges of the British colonies at Halifax and Pensacola. The frontier forts were constructed at strategic locations often where roads and waterways converged. Most of these forts were little more than wooden stockades or blockhouses. The British fort at Ninety-Six, South Carolina, originally built in 1759 as a stockade against the Cherokee Indians, was improved during the Revolution, with sandbags to raise the parapets by three feet.

Some of the forts had been built or refurbished as recently as the French and Indian War. Fort Ticonderoga was a large masonry fort while Fort Stanwix in Western New York was an earth and timber structure. On Sullivan Island, outside Charleston, South Carolina, troops built a large fort from palmetto and oak logs held together with sand.

The British also used fortifications to defend against American attacks. During the Saratoga campaign in 1777, after the first Battle of Freeman's Farm on 17 September, the British and their German auxiliaries constructed enhanced field fortifications, which were assaulted by American forces in the second battle in early October.

In late 1779 with the appearance of French forces and advance of American troops from Charleston, the British garrison at Savannah constructed a series of fortifications. At Savannah, the fortifications were not continuous, but a series of semi-independent batteries deployed in redoubts, arranged in a pattern that covered the avenues of attack, allowing a devastating crossfire from neighbouring batteries. French and American attack columns broke themselves on these redoubts.

Blockhouses were log structures built to withstand attack from any direction. The walls had loopholes and embrasures to allow the defenders to fire small artillery pieces and muskets. They could be two stories in height allowing for greater visibility and firepower.

In addition to forts, the Americans commonly prepared linear field works, typically on higher ground such as ridgelines, and included the use of gabions and chandeliers supporting fascines. Gabions were woven baskets, constructed of sticks and filled with dirt and rocks. Fascines were bundles of brushwood or other material used for strengthening trenches or ramparts, particularly around artillery batteries and used to fill ditches during infantry assaults.

Fieldworks included a wide range of designs. Redoubts typically involved the digging of a trench, creating a dry ditch. The dirt was used to form a rampart. Outside the ditch, large tree branches, preferably dead, called abatis, were positioned with the ends pointed towards the enemy. Often large, sharpened tree trunks, 'frises,' would be embedded into the outside walls of the ramparts.

Redans were V shaped salients extending from a line of fortifications at a point at which an attack was expected but were often open to the rear. Fleches were also V shaped with open back, usually constructed as standalone fortifications. Some fortifications were simple, hastily constructed with wagons, barrels and other material thrown together.

Typically, formal siege tactics consisted of opening a first parallel or earthwork, under cover of night at a range of about 1,000 yards. A battery was then mounted in this earthwork and communications trenches (saps) dug towards the enemy lines. A second parallel and battery were then established at approximately 400 yards. This battery then covered the construction of a third parallel within 75 yards of the enemy. In this situation the defenders assumed an assault was the next step and were expected to enter into negotiations for surrender.

At Yorktown, Crown forces erected a complex line of bastioned works surrounding the town, with additional redoubts and outer works to protect against the approaching allies. Their French and American opponents countered by digging a series of parallel trenches, according to the method described by Vauban. The successful Franco-American assaults on Redoubts No.9 and No.10 left the remaining British entrenchments exposed, leading directly to the surrender of Cornwallis's army.

American Continental regiment defending a portion of extensive fortifications. 40mm Triguard figures.

6

Naval Warfare

Without a navy, the American colonies could do nothing to counter overwhelming British naval presence. With the start of hostilities in 1775, the British used their extensive naval resources to blockade the major American ports, and to bring badly needed supplies and troops from England and raid rebel strongholds. In 1775, the British had only 24 ships in North America, only three with 60 or more guns.

British naval superiority also allowed them to move large numbers of troops at will.

The Royal Navy was able to successfully evacuate the British army from Boston in early 1776 and then transport the reinforced army to land at Staten Island and support the British offensive to force the Continental army from New York. The Royal Navy also operated along the Hudson River supporting various efforts of the army operating in the Hudson Valley. The Navy additionally supported a series of raids on American privateer bases in Virginia and Connecticut.

Until France entered the war in 1778, British naval superiority allowed them to move rapidly at will along the American coast. In 1777, General Howe's use of the Royal Navy to move his forces from New York resulted in great anxiety for the American leadership. When the British fleet disappeared off the coast of New Jersey, General Washington could only guess at its final destination, forcing the Continental army to remain frozen in place until first sightings of the fleet several weeks later. Even then it was unclear exactly where the British would land. The subsequent British landing at Point of Elk was unopposed, allowing the British enough time to establish a base and organise their further advance while Washington struggled to concentrate the American army to meet the threat.

In response to the British naval challenge, the Continental Congress authorised the creation of an American Navy. In addition, Congress established financial incentives intended to encourage American privateers to attack British shipping. These privateers attempted to intercept British supply ships and convoys as they approached British bases in North America. Privateers typically utilised schooners, which were faster and more manoeuvrable, and broke the British blockade of American ports, slipping past the slower British ships of the line. Some privateers operated in waters around the British Isles, taking captured merchant ships to French or Spanish ports. Through the course of the war, 1,697 letters of marque were issued by Congress, individual states or American overseas agents, resulting in the capture of 2,208 British merchant ships.

The entry of France into the as an American ally in 1778 changed the naval balance of power dramatically. Fear of a French/Spanish invasion of the British Isles forced the British to concentrate their naval forces in the English Channel. In addition, the Royal Navy was forced to contend with French naval forces carrying French troops and supplies to their American allies. More importantly, the British navy was required to protect valuable British possessions in the West Indies. All these additional demands on British naval resources resulted in reducing British naval mobility.

In April 1778, a French fleet of 12 ships of the line escorting French infantry under the command of Comte d'Estaing set sail. The French avoided British attempts to intercept the task force, arriving at Delaware Bay in early July. D'Estaing sailed briefly to New York before proceeding to Newport, Rhode Island, where the French were to support American attempts to capture the city. After engaging British naval forces and surviving a major storm at sea, the French retired to Boston. In August, d'Estaing sailed to the West Indies. In 1779, d'Estaing returned to support the Americans in an unsuccessful attempt to capture Savannah.

In July 1780, another French naval task force landed at Newport, Rhode Island with 5,500 infantry, artillery and cavalry under the command of Lieutenant Général de Rochambeau. Unwilling to abandon the French ships blockaded by the British navy, the French remained in Newport until the following July when they marched south with the Continental army to besiege the British at Yorktown. The Yorktown campaign witnessed several naval battles between French and British ships off the Virginia coast. British and French fleets also battled in the West Indies and in the Indian Ocean, supporting efforts to capture valuable trading settlements.

Although the Spanish did not sign a formal alliance with the Americans, they concluded an agreement with the French in 1779. The agreement committed the Spanish Navy and Army to assist the French in attacking British possessions in the West Indies and possibly invading England. In return, the French agreed to assist the Spanish in recapturing the British fortress of Gibraltar.

The Continental Congress established the Continental Navy in October 1775, with the purchase of two armed ships. In December, the Congress authorised the construction of 13 frigates, ranging in armament from 24 guns to 32 guns.

The French contributed several merchant ships for use by American captains. The *Bonhomme Richard* was a former French merchant ship. John Paul Jones took command of this ship in February 1779. The size and armament of the ship made her equivalent, in the weight of its broadside, to two-thirds of that of a 64 gun ship of the line.

The first major operation of the Continental Navy was an attack on Nassau, Bahamas, to capture badly needed gunpowder. An eight-ship task force, with 200 marines, captured Nassau along with the much-needed supplies and two ships in March 1776. Captain John Paul Jones led a raid in April 1778 on the English town of Whitehaven, the first attack on the British home island.

Given the importance of seaborne trade and vulnerability of coastlines, most individual Colonial states formed naval forces. These navies were intended to operate along inland waterways and protect coastal assets.

In 1775, Massachusetts authorised the issuance of letters of marque, allowing private ships to attack and capture British ships. Also authorised was an admiralty court to oversee the disposition of captured ships and supplies. In 1776, Massachusetts authorised the construction of 10 sloops, each carrying 14 to 16 guns. Additional ships were authorised over the course of the war.

Ships

Ships of the line. These were the largest of the sailing ships and carried between 64 and over 100 guns each. The Royal Navy classified these ships as first, second- or third-rate ships. First-rate ships typically carried 100 guns on three decks while second rate ships carried 90–98 guns on three decks. Third-rate ships carried 64–80 guns on two decks. Other types of ships included:

Frigates: Smaller ships carrying 28 to 44 guns.

Brig: two masted square-rigged ship. Carrying 10 to 18 guns

Sloops of war: Fore-and-aft rigged on two or more masts, carrying 10 to 20 guns.

In 1775 the Americans captured Fort Ticonderoga at the southern end of Lake Champlain before advancing north into Canada. American forces captured Montreal but failed in an assault on Quebec and were forced to retreat in early 1776. After the British army was reinforced later in 1776, Lieutenant General Burgoyne moved south in early 1777 to capture Albany, New York. Control of Lake Champlain played a major role in the Canadian campaigns, providing a gateway between Canada and New York.

In May 1775, the Americans captured the schooner *Katherine*, renaming it *Liberty*. By July, after capturing three more ships, the small American fleet controlled Lake Champlain. In addition to using captured ships, the Americans began construction of additional vessels, including row galleys and gondolas. By October 1776, the American fleet had grown to 16 ships including a mix of gondolas, row galleys, schooners, a sloop, a cutter and several bateaux. At the northern end of the lake, the British assembled a fleet, constructed from prefabricated sections brought down from Quebec. These ships were intended to contest control of the lake and protect the British forces as they moved south. While the British fleet included larger ships with crews drawn from the Royal Navy, the American fleet was crewed largely by inexperienced militia.

The various types of ships that composed British and American fleets on Lake Champlain included:

Lateen rigged two masted galleys: The *Washington* was armed with two 18pdrs, two 12pdrs, two 9pdrs, four 6pdrs, one 2pdr and eight swivel guns.

Row galley: Armed watercraft that used oars rather than sails, although many were also fitted with sails.

Gundalow: A flat bottomed sailing barge with three guns.

Cutter: Usually refers to smaller boats with a single fore-and-aft sail.

Bateaux: Small flat bottomed boat mounting cannon or swivel guns.

Gunboats: Small boats with two cannons.

Naval warfare during the American Revolution included both large scale fleet actions and battles between single ships.

7

Strategic Overview and Choices Not Taken

Seas roll and months pass, between the order and execution of plans and the want of a speedy explanation of a single point is enough to defeat a whole system. Edmund Burke.

This section addresses the strategic options considered and plans adopted by British and American leaders during the war. While the American Revolution provides wargamers with many unique and challenging historical scenarios, an examination of other options not taken opens another realm of possibilities. This section includes both a description of the historical options and actions available to each side and notes possible 'what if' scenarios that could be used to generate interesting campaigns or battles.

Throughout the American Revolution the military leadership on both sides began each year developing strategic plans reflecting the current state of the conflict. In the development of these plans various options were evaluated and while ongoing events many times rendered some options obsolete, the plans adopted guided future actions.

British commanders had to reconcile the strategies prepared by government officials hundreds of miles away, typically based on outdated and incomplete information, with the reality on the ground in North America. Under these conditions, British commanders had less flexibility to take advantage of opportunities that appeared during each campaign. In addition to the problems inherent in implementing outdated or unrealistic strategies, the disjointed British command structure hobbled British fortunes. Except for 1776 and 1777 when General Howe's brother Richard commanded the British naval forces in North America, there was limited coordination between the British army and navy, forfeiting a major British strategic advantage; the mobility of movement by sea. While personality conflicts plagued both armies, the impact was more detrimental in the highest levels of British command.

George Washington also had to respond to Congressional oversight and interference, heavily influenced by regional differences, although these directives were made with more accurate information. In addition, given their close proximity, Washington had the opportunity to engage in timely and direct discussions with Congressional leaders.

1775

The conduct of the war by the British leadership in America was hobbled by several factors. Once hostilities broke out in 1775, the British government began issuing a regular series of directives attempting to manage a war that was hundreds of miles distant. Assessments of the situation in America by the British government, beginning with Lord North's government in 1775, resulted in a policy focused on pursuing the conflict by isolating the New England colonies and ignored advice from multiple sources that a war in America would be long and costly. Despite news through the remainder of 1775 that the rebellion had spread outside of New England, the adopted strategy that focused primarily on New England was not modified. A wide net was cast to recruit new regiments in England, Scotland and Ireland. Approaches were also made to hire soldiers, first from Russia and then German principalities, and to unleash Native American tribes on the rebellious colonists.

Believing that a strong military response would bring the colonies to heel, General Howe was dispatched to Boston to assume overall command, accompanied by a trio of generals, Clinton, Burgoyne and Cornwallis, each of whom would play a large role in the war.

1776

The British strategy for 1776 continued to focus on isolating New England and containing the contagion through blockading the seaboard ports, while capturing New York and Rhode Island. Once New York was secured, the British were to move north along the Hudson River to join with an army advancing south from Canada. The two armies would then invade New England and end the rebellion. Howe did not receive these instructions until November and decided to remain in Boston until the spring while the Canadian offensive was delayed until 1777.

As these plans were being developed, Lord North also reshuffled his cabinet. Two ministers who were reluctant to forcefully respond to the rebellion were sacked and Lord Dartmouth was reassigned. Lord George Germain, who advocated for a more aggressive response, was appointed the Secretary for America. Over time Germain took on the role of 'Minister of War.'

In March 1776, Howe evacuated Boston retiring to Halifax to reorganise the army and absorb reinforcements arriving from Europe, before returning to capture New York in August. The British drove Washington's army from Long Island and then north into Westchester County. Howe followed Washington's army into New Jersey, capturing Fort Lee with its large garrison, and forced the Americans across the Delaware River into Pennsylvania by November. Throughout this period, both Lieutenant Generals Cornwallis and Clinton peppered Howe with suggestions for more aggressive action, which were largely ignored, poisoning their relationship.

1777

Despite the reverses at Trenton and Princeton, the British forces in North America were well positioned to begin the new campaign. Naval and land reinforcements were sent in early 1777. Generals Clinton and Burgoyne, who had returned to England in late 1776, lobbied Germain for a larger role in the coming campaign. Refining the previous British government plan of attack, Howe developed a more detailed plan for the 1777 offensive, written in November as the British were still pursuing the American army through New Jersey, and submitted it to Germain for review.

Howe proposed that while New York should be strongly garrisoned, a force of 8,000 should make a diversionary attack towards Philadelphia, hoping to freeze the Continental army in place. A force of 10,000 men would move to capture Newport, Rhode Island before advancing to threaten Boston. At the same time, another force of 10,000 men would strike north along the Hudson River to join with British forces moving south from Canada. With New England reduced by early autumn, the British would turn their attention to Pennsylvania and Virginia, capturing Philadelphia.

Burgoyne, back in London to lobby for command of the Canadian offensive, prepared his own plan proposing that an expedition be mounted from Canada into the Mohawk Valley while the main British army marched south to capture Fort Ticonderoga and then towards Albany, New York. Burgoyne's plan included several alternative strategies. From Fort Ticonderoga, Burgoyne suggested an advance east into the Connecticut River valley in conjunction with Howe's proposed attack on Newport. Burgoyne also raised the possibility that an offensive south from Canada be cancelled and British forces in Canada be transported by the British Royal Navy to support Howe's efforts to capture Philadelphia.

Howe revised his original plan in response to the retreat of Washington across the Delaware River, rising Loyalist sentiment in New Jersey and in understanding that he would not receive the requested reinforcements from home. Prepared on 20 December, Howe dropped both the advance towards Boston and mention of any advance up the Hudson River to Albany. The plan did include a vague promise to support the forces advancing south from Canada, but the capture of Philadelphia would be the primary objective of the 1777 campaign. Howe also recommended that Clinton be given command of the Canadian expedition.

With the American army disintegrating and remaining enlistments set to expire in December, Washington feared the British would continue the campaign by forcing their way across the Delaware. Instead, Howe suspended the campaign and deployed British and German troops into winter quarters, allowing Washington to attack the garrison of Germans at Trenton and defeat British forces at Princeton, reviving American hopes.

An alternative strategy could see Howe deciding to pursue Washington across the Delaware River in late November or early December, possibly capturing Philadelphia.

While Germain was still absorbing Howe's second plan, he was surprised to receive on 3 March yet another revised plan, written after the setbacks of Trenton and Princeton. Howe again requested additional resources and backtracked somewhat on the depth and reliability of Loyalist sentiment but continued to focus on the capture of Philadelphia, mentioning that the 3,500 men he intended to leave at New York might be able to assist the Canadian forces.

At the end of March, Germain approved a final plan that incorporated elements of Burgoyne's and Howe's three separate proposals. Burgoyne was given command of the Canadian forces and instructed to move south towards Albany after sending a detachment into the Mohawk Valley to raise Loyalist and Native American forces that would attack frontier settlements in New York, Pennsylvania and Virginia. The plan proposed that Howe capture Philadelphia but required him to do so quickly so that he could move north to support Burgoyne's advance.

Six weeks later, Germain received news from Howe that he intended to move by sea from New York to attack Philadelphia and in the process relinquish control over New Jersey. Although surprised by both these proposals, Germain did nothing to request a more concrete commitment to coordinating Howe's movements with Burgoyne's invasion. The 1777 campaign began with no shortage of diverging objectives and misunderstandings.

Any of the various plans proposed by Howe and Burgoyne for the 1777 campaign could result in a significantly different outcome to the year. It is not clear why Howe suddenly found the capture of Philadelphia an overriding objective after first proposing that the city could be captured after achieving a junction with the Canadian army and the reduction of New England.

After arriving at Quebec in April, Burgoyne was disappointed to find the response of Loyalists less than hoped. Rather than 2,000 volunteers, just under 700 men were organised into Loyalist units. Burgoyne, like his fellow officers, had low expectations for American volunteers. More disappointments followed. Burgoyne's plan assumed 1,000 workmen and teamsters could be engaged to clear or open roads and transport supplies. He also expected 1,500 horses and 1,000 wagons but could assemble only 500 horses and wagons. The wagons were actually two wheeled carts, which carried only half the load of a conventional four wheeled wagon. Most disappointing was the inability to secure more than 500 Native American allies.

Although Burgoyne began his campaign with diminished resources, he was committed to implementing the adopted plan and assumed Howe would play his role, as he understood it. As 1777 began, Washington correctly believed Howe's main objective would be the capture of Philadelphia. Towards that end, Washington was also convinced that Burgoyne's Canadian army would be transferred south to support Howe. Failing that, Washington downplayed the possibility of an invasion by British forces from Canada unless Howe moved north towards Albany in support.

For his part General Howe moved forward to implement his plan to capture Philadelphia. It is clear he never believed he had any responsibility to support Burgoyne indirectly, let alone by conforming to Germain's plan to move the army north up the Hudson River. In July Washington shifted the Continental Army north and Howe responded by telling Burgoyne if the Americans went to Albany he would follow. At the same time when Washington moved his army into the New York Highlands he did so on the belief that Howe was planning to support Burgoyne.

Once the plans to move the army by sea to capture Philadelphia were put in motion, rather than landing at the Delaware River, Howe once again modified his plan, resolving to sail up the Chesapeake Bay and land in Delaware. Howe delayed his departure until receiving news that Burgoyne had captured Fort Ticonderoga, further supporting his belief that having secured a major objective and a reliable base, Burgoyne would not need his assistance.

While Howe and Washington manoeuvred around Philadelphia, Burgoyne's advance south from Canada became bogged down, and he requested help from Lieutenant General Clinton, in command of the New York garrison. Before leaving on his expedition to Philadelphia, Howe had instructed Clinton that while his primary responsibility was the protection of New York he could use his discretion to decide whether and how to assist Burgoyne, if needed.

As early as April as he was finalising plans for the advance, Burgoyne received a copy of correspondence from Howe, written in April, several days after he had sailed to Canada, maintaining the Canadian army should expect little assistance from him. At that time Burgoyne discounted Howe's position, believing that since George III believed Howe would support his invasion, Howe would eventually be ordered north. By the middle of June, Burgoyne had not only captured Fort Ticonderoga but advanced another 36 miles. Inexplicably Burgoyne remained in place for the next three weeks, waiting for supplies and his heavy artillery train, sacrificing the army's mobility and then took another three weeks to advance less than 20 miles.

While stopped at Skensboro, Burgoyne made the decision to march overland to Fort Edwards rather than retracing his steps to Fort Ticonderoga to sail south along Lake George to Fort George, which would have required a much shorter march to Fort Edward. The decision to march overland required the construction and clearing of forest paths to accommodate Burgoyne's supply and artillery train. The British army spent 10 days at Fort Edward. On 3 August, Burgoyne received a message from Howe unequivocally informing Burgoyne he could expect no help. At this point Burgoyne had the opportunity to abort the campaign but chose instead to push on.

Although Burgoyne now understood he would receive no direct assistance from Howe's main army, he continued to expect some support from Lieutenant General Clinton in New York. Clinton appeared inclined to support Burgoyne as best he could but was firmly committed to protecting New York. Clinton's options to aid Burgoyne were further narrowed when Howe demanded Clinton send reinforcements to Philadelphia, reducing his available manpower.

Burgoyne continued south, crossing the Hudson River at Fort Miller before his advance stalled with the Battle of Freeman's Farm on 19 September. On 20 September Burgoyne received a note from Clinton promising to advance up the Hudson River on 22 September with 2,000 reinforcements. Emboldened by this news, Burgoyne chose not to renew his advance and instead waited for Clinton. Over the next two weeks Burgoyne reinforced his position, reduced rations and waited. During that period Burgoyne convened several councils of war to review various future options but those discussions produced no consensus.

On 3 October another council of war recommended an immediate retreat, which Burgoyne rejected, holding out hope that Clinton was advancing from New York.

Even at this late stage, Burgoyne had a chance to save his army through a retreat to Fort Ticonderoga. Unfortunately, Clinton only began his advance up the Hudson on October 3, but made good progress, capturing Forts Montgomery and Clinton, and forcing Continental forces under General Putnam to abandon his base at Peekskill. While at Verplancks Point, Clinton received a note from Burgoyne detailing his current position and the desperate condition of his army. To Clinton's mortification, Burgoyne also asked him for orders. Clinton was not Burgoyne's superior and was unwilling to take responsibility for Burgoyne's situation. In response Clinton chose to end his advance and return to New York, settling Burgoyne's fate.

Some interesting 'what ifs' can be considered. Whereas Burgoyne's movements conformed to the overall British strategic plan that had been adopted, Howe ignored the basic elements of the plan and appeared to make it up as he went along. The decision to move by sea rather than march overland to Philadelphia consumed too much time and the sea voyage resulted in wastage in men, horses and supply. Howe's sea passage took 32 days, four times what had been initially anticipated and twice as long as an overland march would have taken.

Howe was quite appropriately concerned that a march from New York to Philadelphia would have required detaching resources to protect his lines of communication and supply. Alternatively, Howe hoped for the opportunity to engage Washington's army in a decisive battle, and it is possible that a march across New Jersey would have forced Washington to confront the British advance and offer Howe the battle he desired.

Howe's other error, whether marching overland or sailing, was to wait too long to begin his movement towards Philadelphia. If Howe had initiated the campaign in late spring, he might have defeated Washington and captured Philadelphia by June, allowing Howe to support Burgoyne.

Having landed in Delaware at Point of Elk, Howe had several options, including an advance west to attack Continental supply bases at Reading, Lancaster and York. Washington was always apprehensive of this movement, understanding that the loss of the supply bases could be catastrophic. Washington manoeuvred his army in a manner that allowed him to respond to the possibility of a British attack to the west.

Burgoyne's delay after capturing Fort Ticonderoga allowed an opportunity to push on to Albany to slip through his fingers. American Major General Gates and others believed that had Burgoyne acted with more alacrity he could have won a victory in July.

1778

News of the loss of Burgoyne's army and the subsequent formal entry of France into the war as an ally to the Americans changed the strategic thinking in London, with repercussions impacting on British capabilities and options in America.

Lieutenant General Clinton replaced Howe, whose resignation was accepted. Clinton was selected by default, as General Amhurst refused the appointment, Burgoyne was obviously disgraced, and Cornwallis was still under a cloud for his role in the reverses at Trenton and Princeton. The grim reality that to reconquer the former colonies the

British would need an estimated 80,000 troops forced a reassessment of what defined victory and how it could best be achieved.

Most importantly, the expected entry of France refocused Whitehall's attention on protecting British possessions in the West Indies and in turn Clinton was ordered to dispatch 10,000 troops for service in the Caribbean, Halifax and Florida. In effect, Britain acceded to the loss of New England but believed that by retaining Canada, the western frontier and the middle and southern colonies, along with their Caribbean possessions, the New England states would be surrounded and economically vulnerable.

Clinton was ordered to attempt to force Washington into a decisive battle as soon as possible and to prepare for an offensive in the southern colonies in the autumn. He was also directed to undertake coastal raids on seaports in New England. The reduction in his available forces coupled with the refocus on securing the southern colonies required abandoning Philadelphia in order to protect New York. Clinton retired from Philadelphia, fighting Washington to a standstill at Monmouth.

Although Clinton had been ordered to bring Washington to battle before abandoning Philadelphia, there is no evidence that Clinton realistically considered this option and he did nothing to bring on a general action. Clinton was encouraged by members of the three-member Carlisle Peace Commission to ignore his orders and defend Philadelphia. Washington continued to fear a British attack on the American bases in central Pennsylvania, which would have forced him to confront the British. At the time of his withdrawal from Philadelphia, Clinton commanded an army that would lose 10,000 men as soon as it arrived in New York.

Clinton could have advanced against American supply bases in central Pennsylvania in an attempt to cripple the American army and bring on a decisive battle with Washington's army.

While the British were refining their strategy in the aftermath of the defeat at Saratoga and capture of Philadelphia, Washington was also assessing the strategic impact of those events. In Washington's mind there appeared three realistic options: concentrate the Continental army against Philadelphia; attempt to recapture New York or remain at Valley Forge and react to events as they unfolded.

No less than his British counterparts, General Washington was forced to contend with outside interference. Throughout the war he had to address regional infighting over the appointment of officers, state recruitment and supply of their regiments. Congressional interference centred on military policy. On several occasions Washington had to address Congressional interest in an invasion of Canada.

Members of the Continental Congress, emboldened by the surrender of Burgoyne's army, envisioned an invasion of Canada. The matter was referred to the Board of War, which quickly endorsed the idea and proposed that Lafayette lead the invasion, hopeful that French Canadians would respond sympathetically. Washington was sceptical and worked to undermine the initiative.

Approved in January, the plan called for organising a force of 2,500 men at Bennington, Vermont in February, which would advance across the frozen Lake Champlain to Saint Johns. If the expedition found the Canadian population indisposed to support the American cause, they were to destroy the shipyards and ships before returning to New York. If the Canadians were receptive, Lafayette's army would advance to capture Montreal. Endless wrangling over the proposed command structure delayed the project into March, making it unfeasible.

With news of the French alliance in May, British withdrawal from Philadelphia and the inconclusive battle of Monmouth, the idea of a Canadian invasion surfaced once again. Lafayette continued to promote the idea and suggested a joint operation with the French fleet despite the recent setback at Newport and resulting recriminations against d'Estaing. For their part, the French were uninterested in an offensive directed at Canada. Washington again objected and in addition to the operational problems he had noted earlier he now raised concerns about the larger role of France. He was afraid French control over Canada, coupled with Spanish possessions along the Mississippi River would threaten American expansion. Congress again demurred and the project was dropped.

Congress proposed an American invasion of Canada in February 1778 with 2,500 men under Lafayette, with Laurens as second in command. Later in the year with news of the French alliance, Congress again proposed a Canadian invasion, supported by a French taskforce.

The French delayed the departure of the Toulon fleet carrying d'Estaing's army for two months in 1778. The fleet arrived off the coast of New York at Sandy Hook several days after Clinton evacuated the British army from New Jersey to New York. Had d'Estaing arrived a week or so earlier, his forces, in conjunction with Washington, could have trapped Clinton at Sandy Hook. The French fleet's original destination was Philadelphia and was only later informed the British had withdrawn. Had the French arrived earlier they might also have defeated Howe's fleet as it withdrew from Philadelphia.

With the arrival of the French fleet, Washington and d'Estaing considered their options. Washington wanted to attack New York and although d'Estaing was initially supportive, French naval pilots concluded that the New York channel was too shallow to accommodate the largest French warships. Disappointed, Washington and d'Estaing focused on an attack on Newport. The French initially supported Major General Sullivan's offensive against Newport but after enduring a serious storm and a minor engagement with a British naval squadron, the French withdrew to Boston for repairs. The unexpected French withdrawal doomed the American attack on Newport and forced Sullivan to withdraw, leading to serious recriminations against the French.

Clinton hoped to trap Sullivan's army at Rhode Island in 1778 after the French withdrawal and dispatched a large taskforce to support Pigot at Newport. Pigot, by pursuing Sullivan during his retreat, hastened Sullivan's withdrawal and frustrated Clinton's plans.

1779

Late in 1778, the British unleashed the first phase of their Southern Strategy, capturing Savannah, Georgia. The Southern Strategy was predicated on the belief that Loyalist sentiment was strongest in the south and the presence of British troops would encourage an outpouring of Loyalist volunteers to supplement the British forces. In the north, Clinton – handcuffed by British government war plans – ordered a series of raids down the Connecticut coast and captured Stony Point along the Hudson River, but suffered a humiliating defeat when Continental forces captured the fort and garrison in a daring nighttime assault in July. For the remainder of 1779, he remained largely inactive while British forces in Savanah withstood an attack by a joint French and American army.

Germain, who was delighted with the capture of Savannah in late 1778, urged Clinton to follow up on this victory by extending British control into South Carolina and capturing Charleston. Clinton, who was highly sceptical of the Southern Strategy in general and the assumptions of Loyalist support in particular, responded to Germain's continued interference by requesting he be left alone. He noted that he was on the spot and in the best position to develop appropriate military strategies. Clinton believed that destroying Washington's Continental Army was the quickest way to victory. In addition, he proposed to Germain the establishment of a overall commander in America, responsible for developing realistic military strategies and deploying resources for both the North American and Caribbean theatres. Germain rejected his proposal.

Clinton reluctantly embraced the proposed Southern Strategy and after abandoning Newport, Rhode Island, assembled a large task force and sailed south to Georgia in December to capture the largest prize in the south, Charleston.

Although Washington objected to proposals for a Canadian invasion on several occasions, he did use British concern about a possible invasion to his advantage in 1779. While planning for an offensive against the Indian tribes along the Pennsylvania and New York frontiers, Washington ordered Colonel Moses Hazen to begin what appeared to be preparations for an invasion of Canada through the Connecticut Valley. Hazen ultimately remained in place, but Canadian officials responded by requesting 1,500 reinforcements from Clinton in New York and refused to send aid to their Native American allies when the Americans began their offensive. British fears about a French invasion of Canada loomed large in 1780, with news of the departure of a large French task force.

1780

With the beginning of the new year, Clinton began a methodical campaign to capture Charleston. During the campaign, the simmering disagreement between Clinton and Lieutenant General Cornwallis broke into the open. Not long after the advance began, Cornwallis demanded he not be consulted on any plans to assault Charleston, which Clinton honoured. After capturing Charleston, Clinton assigned Cornwallis command of the southern theatre and left a sizeable detachment as a garrison, before rushing back to New York. Cornwallis waged a campaign across South Carolina, scattering militia units and destroying a reinforced Continental army under Major General Gates

British column on the march.

at Camden in June. Despite these successes, Cornwallis was unable to establish reliable Loyalist control over the Carolina backcountry.

While American fortunes in the south were recovering from the Camden debacle, a French task force under the Comte de Rochambeau landed at Newport, Rhode Island, in July. The French arrival offered Washington an opportunity to explore options with Rochambeau and Amiral de Ternay. Washington quickly raised the issue of attacking New York, suggesting that the French fleet establish naval superiority around New York in early August, followed by the American and French armies initiating a formal siege. Neither Rochambeau nor Ternay were supportive of Washington's proposal, explaining that they both expected additional reinforcements. Ternay was doubtful that, even with the expected reinforcements and possible help from the fleet in the West Indies, an action against New York could not be successful if the heaviest French ships could not enter New York harbour. Rochambeau was also sceptical that Washington could deliver on the 35,000 men he promised to support the attack. The militia might initially turn out, but would they stay if a siege lasted six months or longer?

Rochambeau and Ternay, arriving in the immediate aftermath of the surrender of Charleston, also had doubts about the overall prospects of the American effort. Casting about for alternative strategies, Washington recommended a joint operation in the south. Ironically, after previously stoutly resisting suggestions for an invasion of Canada, Washington also raised that project as an alternative. The French rejected all these options due to continuing concerns that they lacked adequate naval strength.

There are some interesting alternatives to consider at this point. Washington continued to fear a British assault on West Point. Once Clinton's departure from New York to Charleston was known, Washington, with 12,000 Continentals, remained virtually inactive. If Washington had committed his army, supplemented by raising militia, he could have attacked the outlying British defences around New York and threatened the city itself. Clinton, fearing above all the loss of New York, might have been forced to suspend the attack on Charleston to sail north. Washington did not attack New York, nor did he dispatch timely reinforcements south despite continuing requests from Major General Lincoln in command at Charleston.

Furthermore, Lincoln realised, as the British tightened their hold on the countryside and began siege operations, that without significant reinforcements the city would be forced to surrender. Lincoln considered withdrawal on several occasions but was cowed by South Carolina and Charleston officials who threatened to open the city gates to the enemy if the Continentals appeared ready to depart. In early April during a council of war, Lincoln's staff recommended an immediate withdrawal. Washington, when informed that American naval forces would be unable to defend the harbour, remarked that the city should be abandoned, but never passed along any advice or orders to Lincoln despite several requests for direction. Lincoln could have retreated over the Cooper River but would have been forced to fight through Lieutenant General Cornwallis' entrenched forces.

Leslie's invasion of Virginia in October offered the opportunity to ravage the countryside, destroying supply bases and raise Loyalist support. If Leslie had remained in Virginia, he would have complicated the raising of militia and forestalled Virginia militia from marching south to support Greene at Guilford Courthouse. Leslie's actions in Virginia might have forced Greene to march north in late 1780 or early 1781, followed by Cornwallis. Leslie, reinforced by Arnold's expedition in January 1781 and supported by Cornwallis, could have defeated Greene and secured Virginia and the Carolinas.

The big question – should Washington and Rochambeau have invaded Canada in 1780?

In July and August 1780 Clinton developed a plan to attack the French as they landed at Newport. Clinton's plan included the deployment of 6,000 men but required the cooperation of the Royal Navy. Clinton's proposal was rejected by the Royal Navy and the expedition was cancelled.

Ferguson, understanding that the American militia outnumbered his force, desperately requested help from Cornwallis. Inexplicably, perhaps due to illness, Cornwallis sent no assistance.

In September, Cornwallis left a large garrison to hold Charleston and outposts in the South Carolina backcountry and advanced into North Carolina, capturing Charlotte. Major Patrick Ferguson rallied Loyalist troops in the west but was annihilated at King's Mountain in October. In the meantime, Major General Leslie landed at Portsmouth, Virginia with 2,200 men. Leslie had been dispatched by Clinton in response to Cornwallis's request for diversionary actions to keep reinforcements from being sent to North Carolina. His objective was to disrupt communications and intercept or destroy American supplies. News of Ferguson's defeat at King's Mountain resulted in Leslie being recalled, joining Cornwallis who had retreated back into South Carolina. Major General Nathanael Greene assumed command of Continental forces at Hillsboro, North Carolina, in November.

1781

In January, Clinton dispatched another taskforce to invade Virginia. Brigadier General Arnold was given command of 1,600 men and landed at Jamestown. Arnold then ranged into the interior, capturing Richmond and Petersburg before retreating to Portsmouth. Cornwallis resolved to move back into North Carolina after destroying a Continental detachment under Major General Morgan. Lieutenant Colonel Tarleton pursued Morgan but was defeated at Cowpens. Rejoined by the remnants of Tarleton's force, Cornwallis began his pursuit of Morgan's detachment which hoped to rejoin Greene's army in North Carolina. After Morgan rejoined Greene, the American retreat continued, crossing a series of rivers and frustrating Cornwallis' pursuit. Cornwallis believed destroying Greene's army was necessary. After defeating Greene, Cornwallis intended to continue into Virginia, join with Arnold's men to establish a series of strong bases, interdicting American supply lines and cutting off succour to the Carolinas. Cornwallis resumed his pursuit which ended at Guilford Courthouse in March. While Cornwallis drove Greene from the field, the Continental Army survived and retreated south while the British retired briefly to Wilmington before marching north into Virginia.

Alarmed at events in the Southern Department, Washington urged his French allies to commit men and naval resources to support an attack on the British in Virginia. Major General Phillips was dispatched by Clinton with 1,600 men to assume overall command of the British forces in Virginia. After some delay, the French agreed to send 1,000 men by sea in March. Washington assigned 1,200 men under the command of the Marquis de Lafayette to march south in coordination with the French. Chevalier des Touches commanded the French task force, which sailed south towards the Chesapeake Bay but found a British squadron blocking its path at Cape Henry. The two fleets fought an indecisive action but after suffering damage to three ships and over 200 casualties, des Touches broke off the fight and returned to Rhode Island. Lafayette suspended his advance.

In the Spring, Washington and his French allies began discussions about the coming campaign. Washington continued to argue for an attack on New York, utilising the French navy to overwhelm British naval forces and secure New York harbour. Rochambeau rejected an attack on New York, as he had previously, and proposed an operation in the Southern Department. He pledged to march overland if the French navy was unavailable. Rochambeau was informed that a French fleet, commanded by the Comte de Grasse, had been ordered from the Caribbean to North America in mid-summer.

A compromise was reached that committed the joint armies to an attack on New York, pending the disposition of the French fleet. After the agreement was concluded, Rochambeau sent de Grasse, commander of the French fleet, a note instructing him to sail to the Chesapeake Bay rather than New York.

Despite the investment in southern operations, Clinton remained primarily concerned with the potential threat to New York from a combined Franco-American army. Clinton had received information about the discussions between Washington and Rochambeau and was convinced an attack on New York was imminent. Rather than alarming Clinton, the prospect of a decisive battle with the American and French forces offered the opportunity to end the war in a single stroke. Anticipating the showdown, Clinton was inclined to call back troops from the South Carolina garrisons and Cornwallis. With that in mind he was surprised and outraged when he received news that Cornwallis had marched into Virginia. He believed Cornwallis' actions put South Carolina at risk and nothing decisive could be accomplished in Virginia. Specifically Clinton believed Cornwallis placed himself at great risk. Rather than issue orders to Cornwallis to return to the Carolinas or sail to Virginia and either relieve Cornwallis for insubordination or simply send him back south, Clinton took no further action.

After several weeks of fruitless pursuit of Lafayette, Cornwallis retired to Williamsburg. He wrote to Clinton, encouraging him to abandon New York and with their combined forces take full control over Virginia before turning south to destroy Greene. Failing that, Cornwallis suggested Clinton send the Royal Navy to evacuate his forces. Cornwallis waited for Clinton's answer, which was expected. Clinton could not abandon New York without approval from London and he was convinced the American and French forces were about to break themselves on the defences protecting New York. Rather than withdraw Cornwallis' entire army to supplement his army defending New York, Clinton ordered Cornwallis to detach only 3,000 men and fortify his remaining army at Yorktown.

Now that Cornwallis was in Virginia, he and Clinton traded letters through June and July addressing how best Cornwallis should conduct his operations. In late June Clinton recommended Cornwallis march north to Philadelphia, raiding American supply centres before continuing to New York. Four days later another letter from Clinton directed Cornwallis to detach another 2,000 men and retire to Yorktown. A week later Clinton cancelled his previous order, allowing Cornwallis to retain his entire force.

Once Washington and Rochambeau learned that the French fleet was headed for the Chesapeake Bay, preparations were made to march south. To confuse Clinton, the French built large ovens suggesting they were preparing for a long stay while Washington allowed correspondence detailing his plans for an attack on New York to be captured. Clinton was aware of their preparations and despite hoping they suggested an attack on New York, he was not convinced of the ultimate objective of the French and Americans.

On 30 August, the van of the Franco-American forces passed by Staten Island, headed south. British and French fleets engaged in the battle of the Virginia Capes in early September. The battle ended in a draw but while the British commander Admiral Graves vacillated, French reinforcements arrived, deciding the issue and forcing the British fleet to retire to New York. Washington arrived in Williamsburg on 14 September, followed by the combined armies.

Cornwallis had watched with growing concern the gathering of American militia at Williamsburg and as Washington and Rochambeau marched south, he began to craft plans for breaking out from his Yorktown fortifications. Cornwallis considered pushing through Lafayette's defences at Williamsburg before retiring back to North Carolina. Alternatively, he might have transferred the army across the James River to Gloucester Point before marching north.

On 14 September, the day Washington arrived in Williamsburg, Cornwallis resolved to break out from his Yorktown fortifications, recalling his detachment from Gloucester Point and advancing towards Williamsburg to attack Lafayette. On the same day, another letter from Clinton arrived alerting him to the approach of the Franco-American force from New York and promising to send 4,000 reinforcements. Cornwallis, estimating he had enough supplies to hold out until 1 November, cancelled his plans and settled in at Yorktown.

American and French armies began their siege of Yorktown in late September and by the middle of October began to compress British lines. The loss of Redoubts Nos. 9 and 10 on 15 October led Cornwallis to attempt a breakout across the James River to Gloucester Point the next day, which failed due to inclement weather and contrary winds. On 17 October Cornwallis requested terms for surrender.

On that same day Clinton finally dispatched a relief force totalling 7,000 men. Clinton had approved and organised the expedition in September but waited for the arrival of naval reinforcements.

Prior to Guilford Courthouse, Greene held a council of war to offer the alternatives of retreating into Virginia or continuing his army's retreat in North Carolina. Greene feared that Arnold would sail south to land at the Cape Fear River and combine with Cornwallis.

What if the des Touches expedition had successfully landed and fortified Portsmouth in March, followed by Phillips in April?

Could Clinton have evacuated New York and relocated to Virginia or Charleston to carry the war in the Southern Department? Should Clinton have ordered Cornwallis to

American and French advance across the Virginia countryside. 40mm Sash and Saber and Triguard miniatures.

return to North Carolina or evacuated Cornwallis back to New York? Could Cornwallis have marched north to Philadelphia and then to New York in conjunction with a British push south from New York? Should Clinton have dispatched a relief force to Cornwallis in late September? Where would they land if the French fleet continued to blockade the Chesapeake? Could Cornwallis hold out another week and allow the reinforced British naval forces to engage the French blockade?

1782

The war continued through 1782. British, French and Spanish forces fought a seesaw series of naval actions and traded islands in the West Indies. British garrisons occupied New York, Charleston and Savannah. The French fleet found itself committed to operations outside of North America. With only land forces at their disposal, Washington and Rochambeau briefly considered possible actions. Washington again raised the option of a Canadian invasion, which was rejected immediately by the French. Without naval support from the French, campaigns against New York, Charleston or Savannah would be out of the question.

8

Wargaming the American Revolution

Miniatures

The availability of wargame miniatures for gaming the American Revolution ranges from 6mm to 60mm. 28mm appears to be used by a majority of wargamers, based either with multiple figures on a single stand or individually. Individually based figures can be used for skirmish level games or consolidated onto special bases for use in higher level games. 40mm figures used for skirmish level games are typically glued to a single base, but 40mm figures can also be based on multifigure stands.

Figures are available in metal or plastic. While the plastic figures are less expensive, they can require some assembly. Although there are a wide range of manufacturers of miniatures in both metal and plastic, the availability of resin figures has grown with the widespread use of 3D printers.

The attractiveness of the smaller scales allows wargamers with limited budgets and space to game the period. Using either 10mm or 15mm figures can allow for individual stands with large numbers of miniatures.

40mm Sash and Sabre British light infantry compared to 28mm Old Glory British light infantry figures.

28mm figures are widely used for wargaming the American Revolution. Over the recent decade the popularity and availability of 40mm figures has grown. The use of 54mm figures for wargaming the Revolution is also an option, although the availability of figures is somewhat more limited than for the other scales.

The list below includes those manufacturers of whom I am aware. Some of them, like Wargames Foundry, may not currently support their previous figures lines.

Miniatures Manufacturers

6mm
Baccus: www.baccus6mm.com
Adler: http://home.clara.net/adlermin

10mm
Pendraken: www.pendraken.co.uk
Old Glory: www.oldgloryminiatures.com

15mm
Old Glory-Blue Moon: www.oldgloryminiatures.com
Stone Mountain: wargamingminiatures.com
Peter Pig: www.peterpig.co.uk
Essex: www.essexminiatures.co.uk
Musket Miniatures: https://musketminiatures.biz

28mm
Perry: www.perry-miniatures.com
Old Glory: www.oldgloryminiatures.com and www.oldgloryuk.com
Eureka: www.eurekaminuk.com
Brigade Games: www.brigadegames.com
Warlord-Black Powder: www.warlordgames.com
Kings Mountain-Galloping Major: www.gallopingmajorwargames.co.uk
Dixon: www.dixon-minis.com
Wargames Foundry: www.wargamesfoundry.com
Fife and Drum: http://fifeanddrum-minis.com/
Sash and Sabre: www.sashandsaber.com

40mm
Sash and Sabre: www.sashandsaber.com
Front Rank-Gripping Beast: www.grippingbeast.co.uk
Triguard: (formerly Trident): www.triguardminiatures.com
First Legion: www.firstlegionltd.com

60mm
First Legion: www.firstlegionltd.com

Flags

Flag Dude: http: flagdude.com

Flags of War: www.flagsofwar.com

Battle Flag: www.battle-flag.com

GMB: www.gmbdesigns.com

Rules

There is a long list of historical miniature wargaming rules available for the American Revolution. These rules use similar structures for the basing of miniatures, although ground scales and figure scales can vary. Most miniatures wargames can be placed in either the 'big battalion' or 'skirmish' categories. Big battalion games for the horse and musket era use the battalion or regiment as the basic manoeuvre element, while skirmish games can have individual figures that can operate on the battlefield as a group or individually.

Some rules have been developed specifically to wargame the American Revolution while others add modules to a more universal combat system with some modifications to better reflect the unique characteristics of that particular period. Combat and morale are also modelled in a similar manner in most rules, although there can be significant variations in the complexity of the systems. Depending on the scale of the rules some systems aggregate various elements of combat into a single dice roll while others, particularly skirmish level rules, include a richer amount of detail, offering more options for players.

British attack on American positions. 28mm figures. Note number tags on each unit used by the *Carnage and Glory* computer moderated rules for the American Revolution.

I have used the *Carnage and Glory* computer moderated rules for the last 25 years. I have found they include a great level of detail, including reflecting changes in morale and fatigue, in a manner that does overcomplicate the game. They are particularly suited for introducing new players to the period and have a campaign module that is integrated with the tactical system to allow for a seamless resolution of combat when running a campaign. The rules are regularly updated by their author, Nigel Marsh, and continuously supported on a dedicated webpage.

While I am typically a big battalion wargamer and do not play skirmish level games for the American Revolution, I understand that due to financial and perhaps space limitations many wargamers prefer smaller games. The Revolution, like the French and Indian War, is perfectly suited for gaming smaller, skirmish level games. While the big battles of the Revolution are well known there are a wide range of smaller actions that lend themselves to skirmish gaming.

Throughout the Revolution both sides engaged in foraging expeditions intended to both collect supplies and dampen the enthusiasm of the local population to support their opponents. In the spring of 1777, the Americans initiated a foraging operation from their base at Valley Forge involving several divisions. Although Howe initially failed to respond to the American movements, he did attempt to trap a column led by Brigadier General Wayne, which had penetrated New Jersey. Although unsuccessful, Howe's forces skirmished with a collection of Continental and militia units in short but deadly encounters. In the southern theatre large scale battles were not the norm. Rather, smaller engagements were more typical, pitting American militia against British Loyalist units or small detachments of British regulars, typically centred around the capture of isolated frontier forts.

The rules below are those I am familiar with and have seen played at various conventions. The list is by no means exhaustive and there are other rules systems that are not listed here:

> *The British Are Coming*
>
> *Black Powder: Rebellion*
>
> *Sharp Practice*
>
> *Flintlock: Fusilier*
>
> *Volley and Bayonet*
>
> *Muskets and Tomahawks*
>
> *Carnage and Glory American Revolution* Computer Moderated
>
> *British Grenadier*

Terrain

The American Revolution was fought over a wide range of terrain. In the colonies of Massachusetts, Connecticut, Rhode Island, New Jersey and New York the countryside around the larger cities was largely cleared for farming. Stone walls and fences were used to establish the boundaries of farm fields cultivated for crops or used for grazing farm animals.

Example of terrain for the New England and New York battlefields.

Farms featured homesteads constructed of stone or wood, surrounded by a variety of outbuildings, including barns and other storage buildings. Western and northern New York included large swaths of virgin forest, extending along the lakes north into Canada.

In the region surrounding Philadelphia and further west towards Lancaster, Reading and York, the landscape included a patchwork of farms and small villages. Although these areas included extensive farmland, there remained large areas of forest which became thicker near the western frontier.

40mm gaming table for the American Revolution including wheat fields, cornfields, split rail fences and village church.

28mm gaming table, including farm buildings, split rail fences, stone walls surrounding orchards and cultivated fields.

Virginia, North Carolina, South Carolina and Georgia were less densely populated, with smaller towns and settlements. Although Charleston was one of the larger cities in North America, the surrounding countryside was characterised by swamps broken up by numerous creeks and waterways. The land was largely given over to rice farming and other appropriate crops. While large sections of these southern colonies were covered by forests, pine trees composed most of the vegetation. In these pine forests, the trees were widely spaced and the ground under the tree canopy was mostly open, allowing

Typical tabletop battlefield for the American Revolution using teddy bear fur for the base of the table. Teddy bear fur was also used to create the fields and trees pinned through the fur into a foamboard used as the base.

A battlefield layout more typical of the southern colonies with sparse groundcover and a smattering of trees. The use of split rail fences was more typical rather than stone walls to protect fields. American 1st line at Guilford Courthouse, March 1781.

American forces, including militia cavalry, advance against British positions.

formed units to easily manoeuvre. The climate in South Carolina and Georgia coastal areas also restricted the height of most trees.

Split rail fences were used extensively in Virginia and the Carolinas. While fences were typically four to five feet in height, taller fences were used to protect sensitive crops from deer and other animals. Virginia laws absolved the owner of livestock that damaged crops of neighbouring farms if the fences on those farms were not six to seven feet tall.

Buildings

Buildings could be constructed of wood, stone, brick or stucco. Most farms included a residential house, separate kitchen, and several barns and other storage structures. These buildings would be surrounded by garden plots, planted with vegetables, with fences, either split rail or planks, intended to keep out animals.

In the Northern and Middle Departments many residential buildings included extensive use of stone or brick. In the Southern Department and along the western frontier wood was used. The buildings in the Southern Department ranged from palatial plantation houses to very simple log cabins.

Buildings and Terrain Suppliers

Battlefield Terrain Concepts: www.battlfieldterrain.com

Tre Games: www.tregames.com/collections/28mm-structures

Sarissa: www.sarissa-precision.com/collections/north-american-28mm

Charlie Foxtrot: www.charliefoxtrotmodels.com

Things from the Basement: www.thingsfromthebasement.com

9

Wargaming Scenarios

The following section offers several scenarios for wargaming the American Revolution. While the scenarios have been designed for use with the *Carnage and Glory* rules system, I have organised them in a generic fashion and developed orders of battle that would allow their use with other rules.

The scenarios assume a ground scale of approximately 25 yards per inch and a time scale of 15 minute turns. The order of battle includes the estimated troop strength for each unit, which can be adapted to other rules. The basic manoeuvre element is the regiment for infantry, the squadron or troop for cavalry and two-gun artillery sections. Some of the units in the order of battle have been consolidated but they can be broken into small elements if necessary.

While some terrain details are included on the scenario maps and descriptions, most of the battlefields should include split rail fences and stone walls.

Each of the scenarios include an order of battle. The units in the order of battle are located on the scenario map by a letter or number. Those units without a number or letter designation begin the scenario off the board.

Battle of Chatterton Hill – 28 October 1776

Background

During the withdrawal of the Continental army from Harlem Heights, Washington dispatched a large quantity of supplies to the village of White Plains. A network of roads radiated out from White Plains providing communications east through Connecticut to New England and west to the Hudson Highlands.

On 19 October Washington directed Colonel Rufus Putnam, his chief engineer, to examine the country to the north, anticipating Howe's next move. Putnam discovered British forces were within 10 miles of White Plains, where 300 militiamen guarded not only valuable supplies but two crossings of the Bronx River. After reporting his findings to Washington late on 20 October, the commander-in-chief issued orders for a general movement to White Plains. Washington moved his headquarters from Harlem

Heights to Valentine Hill, near Mile Square on 21 October, while Putnam accompanied Brigadier General Lord Sterling's brigade into White Plains that same morning. On 22 October Sterling was followed by Major General Heath's division and then the remainder of General Spencer's division along with Washington. Sullivan's division arrived on 23 October, followed by General Putnam's division.

On their arrival at White Plains, Washington's men began in earnest to construct a line of fortifications, stretching along the heights from the Bronx River, across Purdy and Hatfield Hills to Merritt Hill. Forward of the main line on the plain, Washington constructed a series of earthworks to defend the roads to Dobbs Ferry to the west and Connecticut to the east.

Continental troops advancing through a cornfield, 40mm Sash and Sabre.

As Continental forces continued to concentrate at White Plains, Lee's division remained at Mile Square, protecting the movement of men, artillery and slow-moving supplies from upper Manhattan. Howe divided his army into two columns on 24 October. The right column commanded by General Clinton was directed to move directly towards White Plains while the left column, under Lieutenant General Leopold Phillip von Heister, was ordered to screen the movement of Clinton's column, marching parallel to the Bronx River. Noting Howe's movement, General Lee ordered his division to march to White Plains. Lee's men had to abandon a cache of supplies in order to stay ahead of von Heister's column as both forces marched on opposite banks of the Bronx River. Lee was worried that von Heister's column would attempt to cut off his force, which was encumbered with artillery and over 150 wagons and dispatched McDougall's brigade as a rearguard to protect his movement. McDougall deployed on a ridgeline and was attacked by a strong British force about noon on 25 October and driven back, suffering 20 killed and 40 wounded. With Lee's arrival at White Plains, Washington's assembled force totalled approximately 17,000 and of that roughly 10,000 were militia or militia levies.

Clinton completed a reconnaissance of the American positions at White Plains on 27 October and reported unenthusiastically that the American lines were strongly supported on each flank and the Continentals could easily retreat if necessary. Despite Clinton's gloomy assessment, Howe continued to plan an attack on the American positions. Howe finalised his plan for attacking the Continental army on 28 October.

Early on 28 October, as Howe was directing Clinton and von Heister's columns to begin their attacks, Washington and his staff noted the importance of defending Chatterton Hill, which lay beyond the American lines on the west bank of the Bronx River. Inexplicably, despite occupying and fortifying the ground around White Plains for several days, the importance of Chatterton Hill eluded notice by Washington and others until the morning of the battle. General Lee, accompanying the commander-in-chief pointed towards the hill and told Washington 'there is the ground we ought to occupy.' While still in discussions, Washington received news that the British were advancing towards his lines.

The British slowly pushed forward, Colonel Rufus Putnam rushed to Chatterton Hill, followed by Haslett's Delaware Regiment and two regiments of Massachusetts's militia. Brigadier General McDougall's brigade also climbed the hill, along with a two-gun battery commanded by Captain Alexander Hamilton. The Continental regiments deployed on the brow of Chatterton Hill, behind walls and fences and watched the skirmishing across the Bronx River below. Soon they were joined by Silliman and Douglas' regiments, which retreated across the Bronx and fled up the Hill rather than retire to the White Plains defences.

American forces attack British line. 28mm figures.

As von Heister's column pushed up the York Road, Chatterton Hill loomed on their left, with a line of Continental troops lining the summit. Colonel Johan Rall, commanding a brigade of Hessians noted the American occupation of Chatterton Hill and on his own initiative deployed several regiments across the Bronx River at the base of Chatterton Hill. Howe, suspending his advance just beyond the main American lines, also noted the American presence on Chatterton Hill and ordered Rall to attack the hill while Brigadier General Alexander Leslie's British 2nd Brigade supported their assault. Howe also ordered Colonel von Donop's Hessian grenadier brigade to march from Clinton's column to reinforce Rall and Leslie.

As the fight on Chatterton Hill raged, Washington ordered Brigadier General Beall's brigade of Maryland militia and the 16th Continental Regiment to reinforce McDougall. Before these reinforcements could cross the Bronx River, McDougall's command was driven from the hill.

Order of Battle

American

Key to Map	Brigade: Brigadier General McDougall	
10	Two 3pdrs	
1	1st Connecticut Regiment	180
2	5th Connecticut Regiment	280
3	Brook's Massachusetts Militia	425
4	Massachusetts Militia	370
5	Haslett's Delaware Regiment	310
6	Smallwood's Maryland Regiment	370
7	1st New York Regiment	180
8	3rd New York Regiment	250
9	19th Continental Regiment	230

Reserve

Brigade: Brigadier General Beall

16th Continental Regiment	280
1st Maryland Militia Regiment	400
2nd Maryland Militia Regiment	400
3rd Maryland Militia Regiment	350
4th Maryland Militia Regiment	400

British

Lieutenant General de Heister

I	Four 6pdrs	
	Eight 3pdrs	

Brigade: Oberst von Rall

A	Von Rall Grenadiers	600
B	Leib Musketeers	500
C	Knyphausen Fusiliers	600
D	Von Lossburg Musketeers	600

Brigade: Brigadier General Leslie

E	5th Foot	250
F	28th Foot	300
G	49th Foot	300
H	35th Foot	300

Brigade: Oberst von Donop

J	Von Minnigerode Grenadiers	500
K	Von Block Grenadiers	500
L	Von Linsingen Grenadiers	500

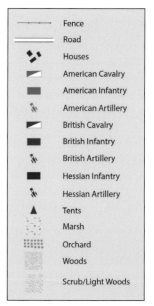

Fence	
Road	
Houses	
American Cavalry	
American Infantry	
American Artillery	
British Cavalry	
British Infantry	
British Artillery	
Hessian Infantry	
Hessian Artillery	
Tents	
Marsh	
Orchard	
Woods	
Scrub/Light Woods	

Scenario Notes

The scenario reflects the situation after the American forces took up positions on Chatterton Hill and Lieutenant General de Heister ordered an assault on the American positions.

Terrain

Chatterton Hill rises 90 to 100 feet above the lower ground along the Bronx River. The face of Chatterton Hill along the Bronx River is very steep and should reduce movement of formed units. There are similar hills east of the Bronx River and south of Chatterton Hill. German artillery deployed on the hill east of the River can engage targets on the top of Chatterton Hill.

The Bronx River is fordable at a location just below the centre of the hill. Troops crossing the River at this location must be in column formation and should be disordered. The eastern bank of the Bronx River is heavily wooded. The west bank, immediately adjacent to the River is also wooded, but the woods do not extend up the slope of the hill.

The crest of Chatterton Hill is bordered by stone walls and split rail fences which provide light cover for defending troops.

Objective

British objective is to capture Chatterton Hill. The American objective is to delay British deployment around the American lines at White Plains. The battle begins at 2:00pm and will end in a draw if the Americans retain possession of the hill at 4:00pm. Bealle's Reserve force is available to enter the table at 4:00pm. Darkness ends the battle at 6:00pm.

Historical Outcome

Howe claimed only 230 casualties while reported American losses were about 175, although likely higher given the two Massachusetts militia regiments, which were the focus of the British attacks, did not provide returns after the battle. It is also likely Howe underreported his losses and perhaps did not fully account for the Hessian dead and wounded. Given their strong defensive position most American casualties were from the heavy artillery fire, while some regiments incurred higher losses during their disordered retreat.

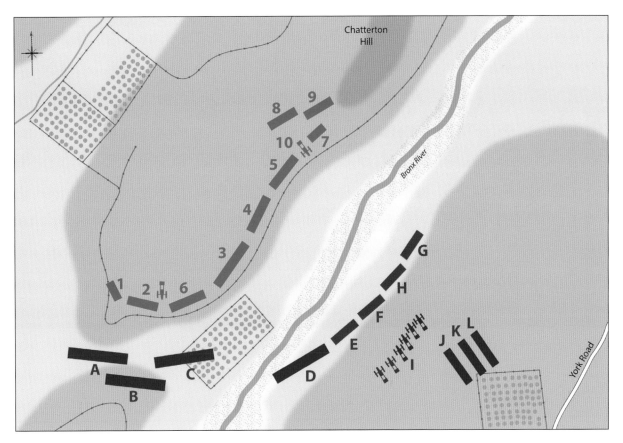

The Battle of Chatterton Hill

Battle of Birmingham Hill – 11 September 1777

Background

On 7 September Howe divided his army into three divisions under Lieutenant General Earl Cornwallis, Major General Grant and Lieutenant General Knyphausen and advanced towards Newark, Delaware and then into Pennsylvania.

Responding to Howe's movements, Washington abandoned his defensive lines along Red Clay Creek and fell back to the Brandywine Creek. Howe received information of Washington's movement and anticipated the coming engagement by reorganising his army again. Howe divided his army roughly in equal parts. Lieutenant General Cornwallis, assigned command of the flanking column, commanded a force made up of British light infantry, grenadiers and guards, along with a Hessian grenadier brigade and the British 3rd and 4th Brigades.

Knyphausen's column, given the role of holding Washington's army in place behind the Brandywine Creek, included the 1st and 2nd British Brigades, the Queen's Rangers, Ferguson's Rifles, two battalions of the 71st Highlanders and a brigade of Hessian infantry. The baggage train, along with supply wagons and herds of cattle were to be left with Knyphausen.

British column on the march, 40mm.

On 9 September both columns moved to Welch's Tavern, four miles from the centre of Washington's defensive line at Chadd's Ford on the Brandywine Creek and then in the afternoon Howe finalised his arrangements, directing Knyphausen followed by Cornwallis, to march to Kennett Square. It was not until early morning of 10 September that both columns approached Kennett Square and only early afternoon when Cornwallis established camp north of Kennett Square while Knyphausen encamped to the east.

Cornwallis marched his column, accompanied by Howe, north from Kennett Square at 5:00am on 11 September led by local Loyalist, Joseph Galloway. At the same time, Knyphausen advanced east along the Great Post Road to Chadd's Ford.

As Knyphausen advanced, Americans under Major General Maxwell fought a delaying action. The British 2nd Brigade moved forward to confront Maxwell's light infantry, which was supported by regiments from Greene's division. Falling back to a final set of breastworks west of the Creek, Maxwell's men put up stiff resistance, before Stirn's Hessian brigade moved forward and at 10:00am Maxwell withdrew his command across the Brandywine.

For the next several hours the American light infantry and British Queen's Rangers and Ferguson's Rifles skirmished along the Brandywine Creek while both sides engaged in desultory artillery exchanges.

Over the course of the morning while Knyphausen was becoming fully engaged with the Americans defending Chadd's Ford, Washington began to receive fragmentary reports of the progress of Howe's flanking column. Sometime after 11:00am Washington began to suspect a British attempt to outflank him and ordered General the Lord Sterling's and General Stephen's Divisions to move north. After only moving a short distance, more conflicting information from the cavalry scouts caused Washington to suspend the movement, but rather than order Sterling and Stephens to return, he allowed them to remain in place.

While Washington vacillated, Howe continued to march, reaching Jeffrey's Ford at 1:00pm. American cavalry on Osborne's Hill noted the movement of Hessian jägers and reported back to Washington. At 2:00pm Washington received the information and immediately ordered Stephens' and Sterling's divisions to resume their march north and directed Sullivan to also move his division north to meet this new threat and take overall command of all three divisions.

After a short rest north of Osborne Hill, Cornwallis ordered his men to deploy into three columns and continue south. The undulating battlefield featured a series of wooded hilltops and ridges connected by fields bordered by fences and stone walls, interspersed by small watercourses that snaked through steep ravines.

The British advance guard, composed of Hessian jägers and British light infantry, watched Sterling's and Stephens' divisions deploying into lines along the crest of Birmingham Hill and moved forward, down Birmingham Road towards the Street Road. Both Sterling and Stephens' divisions had advanced north only to be halted near Dilworth while Washington reconciled conflicting intelligence. When it became clear the British were threatening the American right flank, they were ordered to take up positions on Birmingham Hill.

Sterling occupied the left of the line, Stephens' the right, with five 3pdr guns deployed on level ground between the divisions. While the British light troops were skirmishing with the Americans and the sharp skirmish at the Birmingham Meeting House continued, Cornwallis' main force marched over Osborne Hill and began deploying on the southern slope. The British 1st and 2nd Guards moved to the far right of line while the 1st and 2nd Grenadiers moved forward along the west side of Birmingham Road. Cornwallis brought forward several two-gun sections of 6pdr and 12pdr cannon to support the advance. Left of the Birmingham Road the 1st and 2nd Light Infantry battalions advanced up to Street Road in support of Ewald's jägers. The British 4th Brigade inclined further east behind the light infantry, while the 3rd Brigade remained in reserve. Three regiments of Hessian grenadiers spread out behind the British Guards and Grenadiers on the right.

At the same time Major General Sullivan led his men north through broken terrain along the Brandywine Creek. Realising the British were now behind and below his men guarding the Brandywine Creek fords, Colonel Hazen moved his men south, to

American troops assault Germans defending the cemetery. 28mm.

British infantry cross wheat and corn fields to attack American lines. 28mm.

rendezvous with Sullivan south of the Street Road and falling in with the artillery at the end of the column.

Leaving Brigadier General de Borre with orders to move the division south and east to join the end of the American line on Birmingham Hill, Sullivan rode to confer with Sterling and Stephens. They agreed more room was needed to accommodate Sullivan's men on the left of their line and both divisions were ordered to edge to their right.

Order of Battle

American

Map Key   Commander Major General Sullivan

8	Five 3pdrs	

Brigade: Colonel Stone

	1st Maryland	200
	3rd Maryland	114
	6th Maryland	110
	5th Maryland	140
	Delaware Continentals	110
	Two 3pdrs	

Brigade: Brigadier General de Borre

	2nd Maryland	120
	4th Maryland	200
	7th Maryland	120
	German Battalion	300
	2nd Canadian Regiment	400
	Two 3pdrs	

Division of Major General Stephens

Brigade: Brigadier General Woodford

18	3rd Virginia	150
14	7th Virginia	470
17	11th Virginia	377
16	15th Virginia	200
15	2 3pdrs	

Brigade: Brigadier General Scott

9	4th Virginia	300
10	8th Virginia	157
11	12th Virginia	165

10	Grayson's Additional	100
9	Patton's Additional	124

Division: Major General Lord Sterling

Brigade: Brigadier General Maxwell

1	1st New Jersey	169
2	3rd New Jersey	173

Brigade Brigadier General Conway

3	3rd Pennsylvania	150
4	6th Pennsylvania	200
5	9th Pennsylvania	193
6	12th Pennsylvania	230
7	Spencer's Additional	186

British
Commander-in-Chief: General Howe

Commander: Lieutenant General Lord Cornwallis

B	Two 3pdrs	
	Two 4pdrs	
	Two 4pdrs	
	Two 12pdrs	
	Two 12pdrs	
	1/16th Light Dragoons	60
	2/16th Light Dragoons	58
	3/16th Light Dragoons	57

Brigade: Lieutenant Colonel Meadow

	1st Grenadiers	550

Brigade: Lieutenant Colonel Monckton

	2nd Grenadiers	560

Brigade: Brigadier General Matthew

| C | 1st Guards battalion | 480 |
| D | 2nd Guards battalion | 450 |

Brigade: Brigadier General Abercromby

| | 1st Light Infantry battalion | 320 |
| A | 17th and 42nd Companies | 180 |

Brigade: Brigadier General Maitland

| | 2nd Light Infantry battalion | 520 |

Brigade: Colonel von Donop

	Linsing Grenadiers	425
	Minningerode Grenadiers	445
	Lengerke Grenadiers	420

Brigade: Major General Agnew

	33rd Foot	363
	37th Foot	360
	46th Foot	335
	64th Foot	446

Brigade: Lieutenant Colonel Wurmb

| A | Hessian jägers | 400 |

Scenario Notes

Terrain

The Americans were deployed on a ridgeline covered with medium woods. American troops deployed in the woods gain a cover benefit from the woods. Troops deployed 50 yards or more in the woods are considered out of sight. The slope approaching the American lines is gradual and does not impact on movement. Split rail fences lined the Street Road, and these had an impact on the movement of formed units but not British units in extended order. The Meeting House and the wall around the adjacent cemetery are made of stone and provide cover.

Deployment and Points of Entry

The bulk of the British forces begin off the board. The German jägers and two companies of British light infantry are deployed at the woodlot. On turn 1, the units begin entering the table, in the order identified on the order of battle, between starting location of the British Guards and 3pdr artillery as shown on the map. They can enter in any formation. Sullivan's division enters the table on the far left American flank as shown, on turn 2 in column of march. The order of march should be de Borre's brigade followed by Stone's. Colonel Stone was in command of the division since Sullivan had been given responsibility for the entire American line and had ridden to meet with Stephens and Lord Sterling.

The terrain in the area of Sullivan's entry is broken, with small hills topped with wooded sections that block line of sight. As the lead unit moves onto the table it should be followed by the other units and all must remain in column of march until any of the units are attacked by the enemy.

Objectives

The British objective is to drive the Americans off Birmingham Hill by 6:00pm. The battle begins at 4:00pm and darkness ends action at approximately 7:00pm.

Historical Outcome

The shifting of Stephen's and Lord Sterling's divisions had just been completed when the British began their assault. Lead elements of Sullivan's division, marching through broken terrain, were surprised and attacked by elements of the 1st and 2nd Guards, throwing the entire division into confusion. After a brief attempt to deploy, Sullivan's division retreated in disorder. The collapse of Sullivan's division exposed the American left flank to attack from the British and first Stephens' then Lord Sterling's divisions were driven south towards the American line of retreat. General Washington was able to form a rearguard that stopped the British advance as nightfall ended the battle.

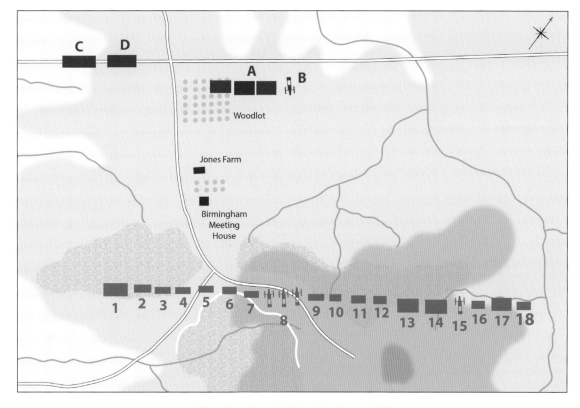

The Battle of Birmingham Hill

The Battle of Camden – 16 August 1780

Background

As the British tightened their siege of Charleston, General George Washington requested permission from Congress to direct Major General Johann de Kalb with the Maryland Line and Delaware Regiment to march south. After Congressional approval, de Kalb moved to Head of Elk on 3 May before reaching Richmond, Virginia on 22 May and then Petersburg. Delayed by a lack of supplies and transport de Kalb divided his force, now including a section of Virginia artillery, into three brigades before advancing to Deep River, North Carolina on 6 July. But by this time Charleston had fallen, forcing de Kalb to halt.

In addition to continued lack of supplies, de Kalb found Major General Richard Caswell, commander of the North Carolina militia, unwilling to respond to his requests to join him and combine their forces. Despite de Kalb's arrival in North Carolina after the surrender of Charleston, American prospects in the Southern Department appeared bleak. In response Washington requested Major General Horatio Gates be appointed to take command of the Southern Department. Gates arrived in Hillsborough on 19 July and continued south to join de Kalb at Coxe's Mill on 26 July.

Gates immediately ordered the army forward, marching through a region depleted of supplies before reaching Masks Ferry on the Peedee River on 1 August. General Caswell finally joined Gates at Deep Creek Crossroads on 7 August and General Edward Stevens with 700 Virginia militia followed Gates by two days. Along the way, hungry American troops were forced to eat green corn and peaches and were issued molasses in place of rum with increasingly ruinous impacts on their health.

In response to Gates' advance, Lord Rawdon consolidated his outposts as he slowly retreated while Cornwallis monitored the movement of the American army from Charleston. On the flanks of Gates' advance, Colonel Charles Sumter attacked British posts at Hanging Rock and Rocky Mount. Although the attacks were unsuccessful, they highlighted the exposed positions of the widely scattered British army and Rawdon ordered the defenders to with. Rawdon gathered his forces at the west fork of Little Lynches Creek, determined to delay Gates' advance and allow Cornwallis to move up from Charleston. Hoping to entice Gates to attack on unfavourable ground, Rawdon retired from the creek to Robertson Place. Gates, wary of attacking Rawdon behind a strong position along Little Lynches Creek, sought instead to outflank him, moving west between 11–13 August towards Rugeley's Mills, 13 miles from Camden. At the same time, Cornwallis marched from Charleston on 10 August and then on to Camden on 13 August.

While at Rugeley's Mill, Gates dispatched Colonel John Senf, his engineer, to explore the ground towards Camden. Senf determined that Saunders Creek, 7.5 miles from Rugeley's Mill and 5.5 miles from Camden would provide a strongly defensible position. Gates' intention appears to have been to occupy strong ground and force Cornwallis to attack on ground of his own choosing. On 15 August, Gates called his officers together at Rugeley's barn. At the meeting, Gates informed the staff of his plan to march at 10:00pm towards Saunders Creek. Marching south, Gates had been led to believe his total strength was over 6,000 and although a significant portion was composed of unreliable militia, Gates was as confident he greatly outnumbered Cornwallis' army of 2,100, dispatching 300 North Carolina militia and 100 Maryland Continentals along with two cannon to reinforce Colonel Sumter. Gates' Adjutant General, Colonel Otho Williams of the Maryland Line, was sceptical of the American numbers and requested updated returns from the officers. Williams presented Gates with this more accurate total as the meeting adjourned. Although surprised at the revised total of just over 4,000 men, Gates dismissed Williams concerns and preparations for the advance continued.

At the same time Gates was organising his advance, Cornwallis, having joined Rawdon, determined that he would attack Gates at his position at Rugeley's Mill. At 10:00pm under a bright moon, both the British and American armies began their march along the Great Wagon Road on a collision course.

At 2:30am on 16 August, the Americans and British stumbled into each other just north of Saunders Creek. After a brief skirmish between American militia and light infantry, supported by Armand's Legion and the British Legion, supported by the 23rd and 33rd Foot, both sides retired.

Cornwallis noted the swamps on both flanks provided his smaller force with a level of protection against having his flanks enveloped by the larger American force and decided to wait until morning to attack. The American position was slightly uphill, and the battlefield was covered by tall pine trees rising out of thick grass but little undergrowth to constrict movement. Gates, surprised that he was opposed by the entire British army, ordered his army to deploy for battle.

Gates deployed the 2nd Maryland Brigade on the right, with the Delaware Regiment close to the road and a two-gun 2pdr section on the far right. Two 6pdr guns were deployed on the road. The North Carolina militia extended on the American left from the road. The Virginia militia extended the line, and the light infantry anchored the far left. Between the North Carolina and Virginia militia, a two-gun 3pdr section

British and American initial deployment at Camden. 40mm.

was positioned. Armand's cavalry was placed behind the light infantry while the 1st Maryland brigade along with two 6pdr guns composed the American reserve, deployed 200 yards behind the main line.

Cornwallis ordered the 33rd Foot, 23rd Fusiliers and light infantry to form on the right of the road, supported by 1/71st Highlanders with one 6pdr gun. On the British left the Volunteers of Ireland, two 3pdr and two 6pdr guns extended from the road, followed by the British Legion infantry and the Royal North Carolina Regiment. Bryan's North Carolina militia formed behind the Royal North Carolina Regiment and 2/71st Highlanders along with one 6pdr gun was posted left of the road as a reserve. The British Legion Cavalry remained in column behind the infantry.

Orders of Battle

American

Map Key   Commander-in-Chief: Major General Gates

Division: Major General Baron de Kalb

Brigade: Brigadier General Smallwood

1	1st and 3rd Maryland Continentals	240
	5th and 7th Maryland Continentals	240

Brigade: Brigadier General Gist

2	2nd and 4th Maryland Continentals	235
	6th Maryland Continentals	245
3	Delaware Continentals	280

Brigade: Lieutenant Colonel Armand

12	Armand Legion Cavalry	60
	Virginia State Cavalry	60
	South Carolina Mounted Infantry	65

Brigade: Colonel Harrison

4	1st Virginia Continental Artillery	Two 6pdrs
5	1st Maryland Continental Artillery	Two 3pdrs
6	2nd Maryland Continental Artillery	Two 6pdrs

Division: Brigadier General Caswell

7	Brigade: Brigadier General Butler	
	Randolph County Militia	300
	Caswell County Militia	300
8	Brigade: Brigadier General Rutherford	
	Surry County Militia	300
	Lincolnton County Militia	300

9	Brigade: Brigadier General Gregory	
	Rowan County Militia	300
	Franklin County Militia	300
10	Brigade: Brigadier General Stevens	
	Pittsylvania County Militia	300
	Louisa County Militia	300

British

Commander in Chief: Lieutenant General Lord Cornwallis

Brigade: Brigadier General Webster

A	23rd Fusiliers	292
B	33rd Foot	230
C	Converged Light Infantry	240

Brigade: Lieutenant Colonel McDonald

| D | 1/71st Highland | 144 |
| E | 2/71st Highland | 110 |

Brigade: Major McLeod

F	1st Company 3rd Royal Artillery	Two 3pdrs
G	2nd Company 3rd Royal Artillery	Two 6pdrs
H	6th Company 4th Royal Artillery	Two 6pdrs
	British Legion Artillery	

Brigade: Colonel Lord Rawdon

J	British Legion Infantry	120
I	Volunteers of Ireland	303
K	Royal North Carolina Regiment	267
L	North Carolina Volunteers	202
M	Brigade: Lieutenant Colonel Tarleton	
	A Squadron British Legion Cavalry	60
	B Squadron British Legion Cavalry	60
	C Squadron British Legion Cavalry	60
	17th Light Dragoons	40

After a bitter struggle in which the American militia fled without offering serious resistance, the American Continentals were surrounded, and de Kalb was killed. After breaking the American army, Tarleton's cavalry continued north, capturing the wagons, cutting down militia, dispersing small units attempting to reform and pursuing the Americans for 22 miles to Hanging Rock.

Scenario Notes

Terrain

The American line is deployed on slightly rising ground, anchored by lower, swampy ground on either flank. Formed units should suffer disorganisation and a movement penalty if moving into these areas. Cavalry is prohibited from any entry into these areas while infantry deployed in extended or skirmish order suffer no movement penalty. The ground on either side of the road is covered by tall pine trees with no undergrowth. The trees do not affect either movement or line of sight of any units.

Objectives

The British objective is to drive the American army from their positions. There is no time limit on the length of the game. If the Americans are forced to retreat from the board while British losses are equal to or higher than American losses, the result would be a draw.

Historical Outcome

The British advance caused the American left flank, composed of militia units, to collapse and retreat, allowing the British to threaten to envelop the Major General de Kalb's division. De Kalb was killed, and the American army dispersed.

The British victory cost 68 dead, 245 wounded and 11 missing. American losses are estimated as 188 killed and several hundred wounded or captured. The losses were most severe among the Maryland line and Delaware Regiment, estimated at 300 killed, wounded or missing.

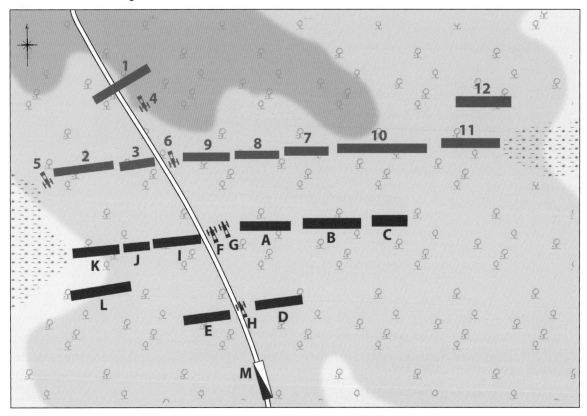

The Battle of Campden

The Battle of Eutaw Springs – 8 September 1781

Background

Major General Nathanael Greene retired from besieging the British garrison at the village of Ninety-Six to the High Hills of the Santee to escape the heat and humidity of the South Carolina summer. After abandoning the village, Lord Rawdon returned to Charleston where, due to poor health, he relinquished command to Lieutenant Colonel Alexander Stewart. Stewart marched out of Charleston and took a position near the confluence of the Congaree and Wateree Rivers, 16 miles from Greene's position.

After being reinforced by a brigade of North Carolina Continentals, Greene marched to Friday's Ferry on the Congaree River on 28 August where he was joined by Brigadier General Pickens with a force of South Carolina militia and South Carolina State troops. Learning of Greene's reinforcements, Stewart retreated to Eutaw Springs on Charleston Road. Brigadier General Marion joined Greene on 7 September as the American army marched to within seven miles of Stewart's position. The British were camped in open fields west and south of a two-storey brick house with a palisaded garden, adjacent to the Eutaw Creek.

Alerted to Stewart's position, Greene ordered an attack on 8 September and at 6:00am the American army advanced along River Road towards the British camp. Despite being alerted to Greene's advance by two deserters, Stewart took no action in response and dispatched a large foraging party down the road towards Greene's army. Lieutenant Colonel Lee's Legion infantry and cavalry, leading the American advance, surprised the foraging party and after defeating a small covering force of Loyalist cavalry, dispersed the group capturing 40 of them.

With this further evidence of the American advance, Stewart deployed his forces in wooded terrain west of the British camp, straddling River Road, with a section of artillery positioned on the road. Greene hurried forward a two 3pdr cannon to support

American troops attack British defending fence line. 40mm

Lee's men while he deployed his force in two lines on either side of the road. He placed the South and North Carolina militia in the first line, supported on the flanks by cavalry and formed the Continental units, including two 6pdrs, in a second line.

Orders of Battle

American

Map Key	Commander-in-Chief: Major General Greene	
18	Two 3pdrs	
19	Two 6pdrs	

	Williams' Brigade: Colonel Williams	
9	1st Maryland Continentals	195
10	2nd Maryland Continentals	180

	Campbell's Brigade: Colonel Campbell	
11	4th Virginia Continentals	150
12	5th Virginia Continentals	150

	Sumner's Brigade: Brigadier General Sumner	
13	1st North Carolina Continentals	125
14	2nd North Carolina Continentals	130
15	3rd North Carolina Continentals	120

	Pickens' Brigade: Brigadier General Pickens	
1	South Carolina State Regiment	75
2	South Carolina State Dragoons	70
3	South Carolina Militia	307
4	North Carolina Militia	150

	Marion's Brigade: Brigadier General Marion	
5	South Carolina Partisan Infantry	200
6	South Carolina Partisan Cavalry	40

	Lee's Brigade: Colonel Lee	
7	Lee's Legion Infantry	60
8	Lee's Legion Cavalry	100

Washington's Brigade: Lieutenant Colonel Washington

| 16 | 1st/3rd Continental Dragoons | 85 |
| 17 | Delaware Continentals | 70 |

British

Commander-in-Chief: Lieutenant General Stewart

| K | Two 6pdrs |
| L | One 3pdr |

Dawson's Brigade: Major Dawson

B	3rd Foot	340
G	63rd Foot	95
H	64th Foot	180
C	2/84th Highland	80

Cruger's Brigade: Lieutenant Colonel Cruger

D	1st De Lancey's	75
E	New Jersey Volunteers	60
F	New York Volunteers	75

Marjoribanks Brigade: Major Marjoribanks

| A | 3rd/19th/30th Grenadier Companies | 140 |
| | 3rd/19th/30th Light Infantry Companies | 140 |

Coffin's Brigade: Major Coffin

| I | Provincial Light Infantry | 110 |
| J | Loyalist Mounted Infantry | 70 |

Scenario Notes

The scenario begins at 8:00am with the Americans advancing towards the British line.

Terrain

The battlefield terrain is largely open, with widely scattered pine trees. The creek is lined with dense hedges that provide medium cover to defending units. The British camp is bordered by split rail fences providing light cover from musket fire but no cover from artillery fire. The house is made of brick and should be considered a strongpoint. The garden attached to the house is palisaded with a tall fence that provides medium cover.

Objective

The American objective is to force the British from their position.

Historical Outcome

The Americans advanced against the British line, pushing them back towards their camp. A portion of British forces retired to the plantation house and garden, which withstood several American assaults. The remainder of British forces retreated though their camp while the American pursuit became disordered after the Continentals began looting the British camp.

Concerned about a British counterattack, Greene ordered a retreat, securing the wounded and withdrawing to Burdell's Plantation. Previously unengaged militia cavalry, joined by the remnants of Washington's command covered the retreat, driving back several charges from the Loyalist mounted infantry.

American losses were 139 killed, 375 wounded and 74 missing, while the British reported 85 killed, 350 wounded and 257 missing.

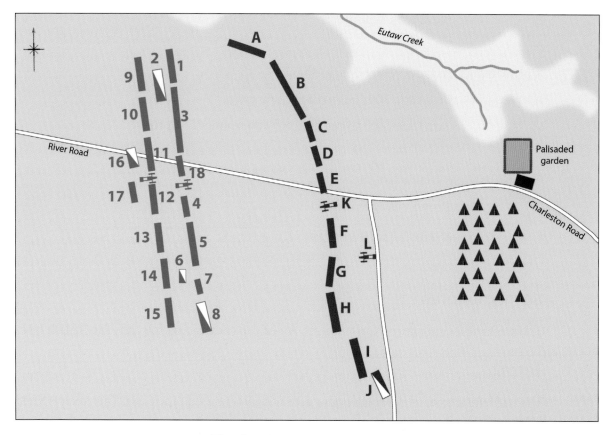

The Battle of Eutaw Springs

Battle of Green Springs – 6 July 1781

Background

In late June 1781, Cornwallis slowly retired towards Williamsburg, followed closely by Major General de Lafayette. After receiving orders from General Clinton to suspend his offensive operations in Virginia and detach a portion of his force to reinforce British troops in New York, Cornwallis hoped to strike at Lafayette before returning to Portsmouth. Cornwallis marched from Williamsburg on 4 July, headed towards Jamestown, intent on crossing the James River. On 6 July, after sending the Queen's Rangers and baggage across the River, Cornwallis deployed the bulk of his army out of sight, south of the Harris Plantation, two miles northeast of the ferry crossing. Cornwallis hoped that he could entice Wayne's command, which was leading the American advance, into a precipitous attack on what appeared to be a small British rearguard. Cornwallis hoped he could trap Wayne's advance guard and force Lafayette to commit his main force in an uneven battle.

On 6 July Wayne paused at the Green Springs Plantation at 2:00pm, before moving along a causeway towards the British pickets deployed around the Harris Plantation. He advanced with a mixed force that included militia riflemen and cavalry, along with Pennsylvania Continentals and light infantry plus three 6pdr cannon. At 3:00pm Wayne's men moved along a raised causeway surrounded by cleared marsh ground on either side. As Wayne advanced, Lafayette (still unconvinced of the British retreat) moved to the James River and after seeing only Simcoe's men on the opposite bank, rushed back to Green Spring Plantation hoping to stop Wayne's advance. Finding Wayne already engaged and the 2nd and 3rd Pennsylvania Regiments moving forward in support, he deployed two light infantry battalions at the Green Springs Plantation before hurrying forward.

American defending in two lines. 40mm figures.

Order of Battle

American

Map Key   Commander-in-Chief: Marquis de Lafayette

Major General Wayne

Advance Force
Colonel Mercer

3	McPherson Legion Light Infantry	50
2	McPherson Legion Cavalry	40

Major Galvan

1	Virginia Militia Rifle	150
4	2nd Light Infantry: Two Companies	80

Main Force
Major Wyllys

5	2nd Light Infantry	200
	Virginia Light Infantry	150

Colonel Humpton

9	One 6pdr	
10	One 6pdr	
11	One 6pdr	
6	1st Pennsylvania	200
7	2nd Pennsylvania	210
8	3rd Pennsylvania	250

Reserve Force
Colonel Voss

12	1st Light Infantry	300
13	3rd Light Infantry	300

British

Commander-in-Chief: Lieutenant General Cornwallis

Left Wing
Lieutenant Colonel Dundas

A	43rd Foot	280
B	80th Foot	500

| C | 76th Foot | 520 |
| D | British Legion Cavalry | 250 |

Right Wing
Lieutenant Colonel Yorke

L	Two 6pdrs	
G	33rd Foot	230
H	23rd Fusiliers	225

Lieutenant Colonel Abercromby

| E | 1st Light Infantry | 490 |
| F | 2nd Light Infantry | 350 |

Brigadier General O'Hara

I	1st Guards	260
J	2nd Guards	250
K	Von Bose Musketeers	340

Scenario Notes

Terrain

The Greenspring battlefield is generally flat, composed of open fields and thickly wooded areas. Movement through the woods should be reduced for formed units. The Harris and Wilkinson Plantations include a main house and surrounding outbuildings, with attendant gardens surrounded by split rail fences.

American deployment at Green Springs. 40mm figures.

Deployment

The British first line for both wings can move on the first turn. The units in the second line are out of sight, either deployed in the woods or in a swale, screened by the units of the first line. The American advance force should start the game deployed at the Harris Plantation and the main force at the edge of the woods behind the Plantation. The American reserve force of the 1st and 3rd Light Infantry battalions can enter the table at the location shown in march column, no earlier than turn 6.

Objectives

The battle begins at 4:00pm. The British objective is to destroy the American forces. The American objective is to withdraw in good order. The American forces cannot voluntarily withdraw from their starting positions until units from the British second line advance out of their protected positions.

Historical Outcome

Although initially surprised by the British deployment and attack, Major General Wayne ordered an American advance which stalled under heavy British fire. The American attack delayed the British advance, which was then slowed by American fire. Despite abandoning two cannon, Wayne was able to retire successfully to Green Springs Plantation. Darkness put an end to the battle, with the Americans suffering 28 dead, 95 wounded and nine missing and the British 11 dead and 66 wounded.

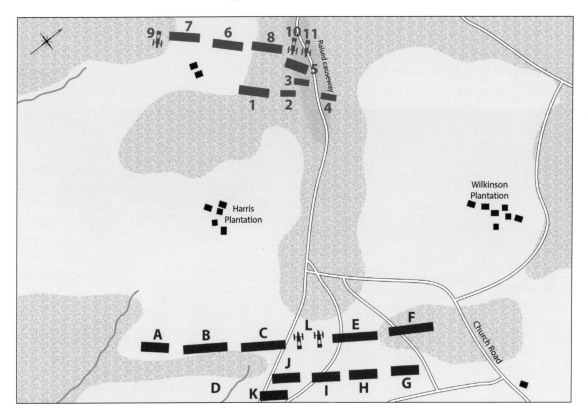

The Battle of Green Springs

Bibliography

Berg, Fred Anderson, *Encyclopaedia of Continental army Units*, Stackpole Books, Harrisburg PA, 1972

Chartrand, Rene and Back, Francis, *The French army in the American War of Independence*, Osprey, London, 1991.

Chartrand, Rene, *American Loyalist Troops 1775–1784*, Osprey, London, 2008

Elting, John, editor, *Military Uniforms in America, The Era of the American Revolution 1755–1795*, Presidio Press, San Rafael, CA 1974.

Hogg, Ian V. and Batchelor, John H., *Armies of the American Revolution*, Prentice Hall, New Jersey, 1975.

Katcher, Phillip, *Uniforms of the Continental Army*, George Sumway Publisher, York, PA 1981

Katcher, Phillip, *Encyclopaedia of British, Provincial and German army Units 1775–1783*, Stackpole Books, Harrisburg, PA 1973

May, Robin and Embleton, Gerry, *The British army in North America 1775–1783*, Osprey, London, 1997

Milsop, John, *Continental Infantryman of the American Revolution*, Osprey, London, 2004

Mollo, John and McGregor Malcom, *Uniforms of the American Revolution*, MacMillian Publishing, New York 1775

Novak, Greg, *The American War of Independence, Book One, the Northern Campaigns*, Old Glory, Calumet, 2001.

Novak, Greg, *The American War of Independence, Book Two, the Southern Campaigns*, Old Glory, Calumet, 2001.

Richardson, Edward W. *Standards and Colours of the American Revolution*, University of Pennsylvania Press, 1982

Smith, Digby and Kiley, Kevin, *Uniforms from 1775–1783 The American Revolutionary War*, Lorenz Books, London, 2008

Spring, Matthew H., *With Zeal and Bayonets Only*, University of Oklahoma Press, Norman OK 2008,

Troiani, Don and Kochan, James, *Soldiers of the American Revolution*, Stackpole Books, Mechanicsburg PA 2007

Wright, Robert K., *The Continental Army*, Centre of Military History United States Army, Washington DC, 1983

Young, Peter, *George Washington's Army*, Osprey, London, 1972

Zlatich, Marko and Copeland, Peter F., *General Washington's army 1: 1775–1778*, Osprey, London, 1994

Zlatich, Marko and Younghusband, Bill, *General Washington's army 2: 1779–1783*, Osprey, London, 1995.

About the author

David Bonk is a long-time wargamer, military history author and student of the American Revolution. He is a former Board member of the Historical Miniatures Gaming Society (HMGS), award-winning gamemaster and 2019 HMGS Gamemaster of the Year. In addition to wargaming the American Revolution Bonk also has collected extensive miniatures and games in a wide range of periods including medieval, Eastern Renaissance, Great Northern War, Napoleonic, American Civil War, WWII and Vietnam.

David is also the author of Helion's *Atlas of the Battles and Campaigns of the American Revolution 1775-1783* (ISBN 978-1-914059-79-7)

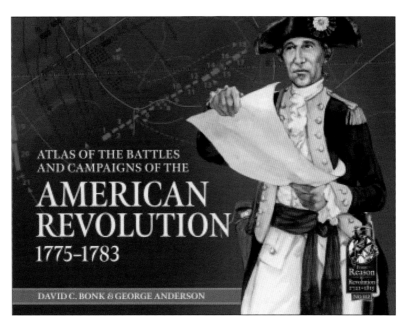

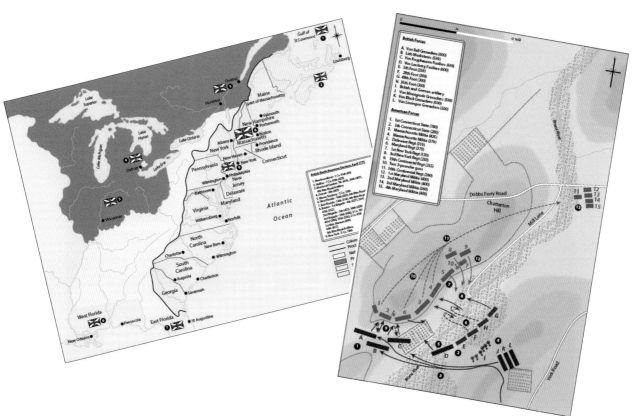

HELION WARGAMES

Helion Wargames has been created to give the gamer a new range of books and downloads offering introductions to the many periods covered by the company's book series and beyond. Whilst we will be publishing rules systems, the series will focus mainly on primers and introductions to new historical periods and figure scales. Working with writers and gamers from within the wargaming industry, Helion Wargames aims to provide both novice and veteran hobbyist alike with inspiration and help in getting the most from their games.

www.helion.co.uk/series/helion-wargames.php